"My survival kit is now complete with Jeffery Self's hilarious new book! I feel more confident and educated, and frankly, safer among heterosexuals now after reading this guide book!"

"I've always claimed that Jeffery Self is the funniest writer and performer of his generation. *Straight People* is the hilarious LOL nail in any counter-argument coffin. Because I'll kill anyone who disagrees."

"What Jeffery Self knows about straight people would fit in a book. I laughed a lot and learned a great deal. It's the literary equivalent of a rectal examination."

"People always say that Jeffery Self is the poor man's Kristen Johnston, but that's not only untrue, it's offensive to both of us. He's quite clearly the poor man's Amy Sedaris."

"Jeffery Self is hilarious. His originality and wit blow me away every time!"

"Jeffery's humor combines old-guard theater queen sophistication with 21st century irreverence—and his work often re̶d̶̶ rs of laughter."

Straight People

A Spotter's Guide to the Fascinating
World of Heterosexuals

Jeffery Self

RUNNING PRESS
PHILADELPHIA · LONDON

3 1357 00154 9895

Books published by Running Press are available at special discounts for bulk purchases in the United States by corporations, institutions, and other organizations. For more information, please contact the Special Markets Department at the Perseus Books Group, 2300 Chestnut Street, Suite 200, Philadelphia, PA 19103, or call (800) 810-4145, ext. 5000, or e-mail special.markets@perseusbooks.com.

ISBN 978-0-7624-4897-5
Library of Congress Control Number: 2012944545

E-book ISBN 978-0-7624-4898-2

9 8 7 6 5 4 3 2 1
Digit on the right indicates the number of this printing

Cover and interior design by Jason Kayser
Edited by Jordana Tusman
Typography: Concorde, Helvetica, and Sketchetik

Running Press Book Publishers
2300 Chestnut Street
Philadelphia, PA 19103-4371

Visit us on the web!
www.runningpress.com

Dedication

To my parents, two of the coolest Heterosexuals I've ever met. And to Patrick, my bug.

Contents

Here we'll get to know each other, like really get to know each other. Know what I mean? No. Not like that. Geez. Get your mind out of the gutter. This is a book, for crying out loud!

This chapter outlines the varied breeds within the Heterosexual species. From Hipsters to Married Couples to Sassy Black Ladies, refer to this chapter while Heterosexual Watching to determine what kind of Heterosexual you've spotted.

An explanation of the diverse habitats of the Heterosexual, from those found in metropolitan cities to those living a quieter life in suburbia.

An exploration of the quirky habits practiced by Heterosexuals, from their gender-specific watering holes (called Straight Bars) to their distinctive mating rituals (known as dating).

Introduction

What Is a Heterosexual?

HELLO, HETEROSEXUAL WATCHERS, STRAIGHT-PEOPLE SPOTTERS, and Opposite-Sex-Couples Enthusiasts! My name is Jeffery Self, and, yes, that is a real name.

I know what you're thinking: The name *Self* sounds about as made up as *Whoopi Goldberg*, but you're wrong. *Self* is my given name, but while we're on the topic: *Whoopi Goldberg* is the most ridiculous of made-up names in the history of such a thing. Especially when you consider that her real name is Caryn Elaine Johnson. I think that I seem more like a Caryn Elaine Johnson than Whoopi Goldberg does, but none of this has anything to do with Heterosexuals except that Whoopi is one of them–but enough about Whoopi;* let's get back to my book, shall we?

....

*Not going to lie: This isn't the last time you're going to read about Whoopi. In this book, I will be exposing you to the fascinating world of Heterosexual Watching. Some of you might be scratching your heads. If so, first of all, wash your hair and maybe it wouldn't itch so much, and, second of all, let me explain.

What Is Heterosexual Watching?

het·er·o·sex·u·al watch·ing

noun. 1. The hobby of watching and observing the endlessly varied species of the Heterosexual, also known as Straight People. 2. The practice of observing this marvelous species that has been called "common," "prevalent," and "capable of reproduction."

Now, you might be wondering about me. That's to be expected because, well, I'm endlessly fascinating. You're probably asking yourself or your significant other, or your Wilson soccer ball with a face drawn on it if you're Tom Hanks in *Cast Away*, *why* should I learn about Straight People from *this guy*?! He seems like a total D-bag, and Jeffery Self is maybe the stupidest name I've heard since Meryl Streep named her daughter Mamie Gummer. What authority does this *Jeffery* freaking *Self* have to tell me anything about anything? *Especially Straight People?*

That is a totally valid question, and I'm happy to answer it if you'd lower your voice, lighten your tone, and leave Meryl Streep's immediate family out of this. Here are 10 of my qualifications that you should know before we get started:

1. I live in Los Angeles, where some of the world's most famous Heterosexuals reside. In my short time here I've seen: Emily VanCamp shopping for a mattress, the guy from *Entourage* eating a Chinese chicken salad at a restaurant, and even Kirstie Alley standing in a shop window staring at traffic with a look that either said, "I have been wronged by the world one too many times" or "I am Kirstie Alley."

2. Not only was I raised by a Heterosexual. I was raised by *two* Heterosexuals.

3. I live in an apartment building where Heterosexuals live. In fact, I've heard my Heterosexual upstairs neighbor having sex more times in the past month than I've had all year.

4. I'm gay. Which means I know everything about pop culture and that I can sing the words to *every* Spice Girls song that has ever been recorded. And guess who are *all* Heterosexuals? That's right: the Spice Girls. With the exception of Scary Spice; she seems like she could go either way.

5. I made out with *a lot* of Straight Guys in college.

6. There is no such thing as a Jennifer Aniston movie that I've never seen.

7. I'm medicated nowadays, so I'm *a lot* less to deal with on a daily basis.

8. My boyfriend works at a women's daytime talk show, and we get *a lot* of free women's lotion and bath products, so I basically smell like your girlfriend. Or more like your aunt Gwen. Who might also be your girlfriend. I don't know your personal life and I don't need to. Speaking of which . . .

9. I don't judge. Seriously. I don't. Except if you're a serial killer, a con artist, or Julianna Margulies.

10. And finally: I've been around Heterosexuals my whole life. Some of my favorite people are Heterosexuals, and I've closely studied their uniquely fascinating behavior–from Beer Pong to girls' nights to the quirky ways they attract their mates–and I've compiled all these discoveries into this spotter's guide. *Plus*, I know what Tina Fey smells like!

Now that you know who I am, it's my turn to figure out who the hell *you* are. If you're reading this book, that likely means you're one of three kinds of people:

1. You, yourself, are a Heterosexual Watcher and are purchasing this spotter's guide to aid you in your Heterosexual-Watching expeditions. If so, hello, my brethren. Whether you're a full-time Heterosexual Watcher or merely an armchair hobbyist, I firmly believe this spotter's guide will prove helpful to you, and I'm honored to be included in your Heterosexual-Watching adventures.

2. You *are* a Heterosexual and are intrigued to learn more about the species you belong to. Right on! I love learners!

3. You are my mom. Hey, Mom! Great blouse! Chico's,* right?

---

*Chico's is an extremely popular shopping destination among Heterosexual Moms. This chain of shops is known for its flowing fabrics, chunky jewelry, and totally insane commercials in which middle-aged women say, "It was a Chico's kind of day."

FAQs about Heterosexuals

As you read this book you will probably be met with a lot of burning questions. Questions like: What do I need to Heterosexual-Watch? Where do I go to Heterosexual-Watch? Am I a Heterosexual? Are you going to finish that blueberry crumble muffin? Fear not: In the following pages, I will be answering all these questions and more. However, I will not be answering that last question because, *duh*, I'm going to finish it, and if I'm being honest, I find it kind of rude that you'd even ask me before I've even taken my first bite, but whatever. Here are some frequently asked questions.

Where do I go to Heterosexual-Watch?

Heterosexual Watching can be done in pretty much every climate and on every continent. Any major city can serve as a great watching spot. However, centralized sections—such as the Castro District in San Francisco or Chelsea in New York City or a Kathy Griffin stand-up comedy show—are proven to be far more difficult than say, Chattanooga, Tennessee.

How do I know if Heterosexual Watching is for me?

You don't, but just as with anything else in life (except for eating wet dog food or wearing men's Spanx), you won't know until you try.

What type of clothing is recommended for Heterosexual Watching?

It is best to wear something that will blend in. Just as hunters wear camouflage in the forest, a Heterosexual Watcher should attempt to blend into Heterosexual surroundings. You can achieve this by sporting Heterosexual clothing, such as a Mets cap, tapered jeans, a woman's peasant blouse (only if you're a female, of course—sorry, fellas), overalls (but remember to wear a shirt underneath, unless you're Heterosexual Watching in the Deep South or you're in an amateur production of *Oklahoma!*), sweatpants that have things such as *Juicy*, *Pink*, or *Mama's Behind* written on the butt (again, ladies only), novelty T-shirts, and jackets made by Carhartt.

Should I eat before going Heterosexual Watching?

It isn't required, and, in some cases, it's not recommended. A great way to entice Heterosexuals into speaking to you is by inviting them out for a meal. A great Heterosexual once said, "I don't trust a man until I sit down to dinner with him." And that great Heterosexual was none other than Jared from Subway.

Do I know a Heterosexual?

With the exception of those working in musical theater and/or attending Sarah Lawrence, the answer is most likely yes.

10 Signs That You Are a Heterosexual

1. That man standing next to you is your husband.

2. You fear you'll never live up to your mother-in-law's expectations.

3. You own a Snuggie.

4. You saw *The Vow*. In theaters.

5. You know the lyrics to any song by Train.

6. You have unironically laughed at Dane Cook.

7. You've ever been late to dinner at Outback Steakhouse because of your children.

8. You had a poster of Zac Efron in your bedroom during the first decade of the 21st century, and you are not a 30-year-old man.

9. You've given serious thought to ordering a pair of those pajama jeans.

10. You've used the term *chillax* within the past two years.

Are Heterosexuals ever attracted to people of the same sex?
Heterosexuals are attracted to people of the opposite sex; that is what distinguishes them as Heterosexuals. However, even Heterosexual Males find photos of young Brad Pitt to be jaw-dropping and mesmerizing. If they say they don't, they're lying to you.

How do I know if I'm a Heterosexual?
There are many ways to find out if you're a Heterosexual. For one, try kissing a member of the opposite sex and see how you feel afterward. If you're turned on, you might be a Heterosexual. If you feel like you just licked an elephant's butt, you probably aren't.

I currently identify as a Heterosexual, but sometimes I'm not so sure. How do I know if I'm not a Heterosexual after all?
Just as you can figure out whether or not you *are* a Heterosexual, there are many warning signs to help you figure out if you're *not* one. The most effective method tends to be watching the movie *Beaches* and seeing how you feel afterward. However, sometimes that isn't clear enough. Take a look at these 10 most common warning signs that you are *not* a Heterosexual.

10 Signs That You Are *Not* a Heterosexual

1. When I mention *Dorothy Loudon*, you know whom I'm talking about.

2. The majority of your shirts are sleeveless.

3. You use your iPhone for Grindr more than for actually making calls.

4. You've ever wondered, "Why hasn't Mo'Nique made another movie since *Precious*?"

5. You follow Jackée Harry on Twitter.

6. You have a favorite episode of *Designing Women*.

7. The distressed jeans you're wearing came like that.

8. You are a hairdresser named Richard.

9. You drink rosé.

10. You've ever "put your paws up" or called yourself a "little monster."

My gym buddy is a Heterosexual, and I'm always worried that I might say the wrong thing. Is there a "wrong thing to say to Heterosexuals"?

Yes, but that's a difficult question to answer and relies heavily on the situation you're in. If you're in, say, a sauna with your Heterosexual gym buddy, you probably shouldn't say something like, "I've seen *a lot* of movies that start out like this," no matter how many movies you've seen that actually start out like that. However, you're more than welcome to say, "Did you like *The King's Speech*? I didn't." He will most certainly agree, and you can spend the rest of your gym visit discussing how overrated Helena Bonham Carter is—a subject anyone can relate to.

Where do Heterosexuals come from?

Sometime around the evolution of man came the evolution of woman. Seeing as there was literally *nothing* to do back then (literally, like not even TiVo), the Heterosexual Male and Female started to occupy their time with casual hookups and eventually reproduction; from there, an army of Heterosexuals were born and continue the Heterosexual lifestyle to this very day.

Have we ever had a Heterosexual president?

A few, yes. But it's hard to say specifically which ones.

I am not a Heterosexual, but sometimes I find myself staring at attractive Heterosexuals in public places. Is that considered Heterosexual Watching?

There is a fine line between checking someone out and the hobby of Heterosexual Watching. Who among us hasn't admired a gorgeous married man pushing a grocery cart through the store and buying baby formula? With the exception of lesbians and people who hate babies, everyone has. An attractive fella is an attractive fella, no matter whose team he's batting for. The same goes for the ladies. But just because you're staring at some hot guy for the second day in a row at Starbucks, and just because he's wearing a baby blue–striped tank top today and his pecs are even better than you imagined they would be underneath that American Apparel V-neck he wore yesterday, and just because you keep looking for excuses to turn around and admire his physique, going so far as to spill an entire Greek yogurt parfait on the (very annoyed) woman next to you just so he might get up and offer you a napkin does *not* qualify as Heterosexual Watching.

In such an instance, you are politely admiring the male form or creeping that guy out. Heterosexual Watching is a much more nuanced study of the species and goes *much* deeper than wondering if said hot Heterosexual guy in Starbucks, whom I've started calling Billy Santiago by the way, wears boxers or briefs, and whether Billy Santiago lives around here or whether he came back to this Starbucks today in that very revealing tank top to let me know he noticed me, too. Did he?

So, no, Heterosexual Watching is *not* that. It's a far more serious hobby.*

Let's set some ground rules now.

---

*If you don't think you're cut out for the world of Heterosexual Watching, might I suggest other hobbies I enjoy, including record collecting, reading memoirs, collecting Beanie Babies, going to therapy, hanging out at those $30 Thai massage places just to feel the touch of another human, or eating snacks!

Heterosexual-Watching Rules

1. While Heterosexual Watching, it is *vital* to respect Heterosexuals, their environment, and their lifestyle. Heterosexuals are generally a loving and amicable species, and in order for all of us to live happily as one, we must respect each other's quirky habits and ways. Just because you don't "get" Natalie Portman doesn't mean the Heterosexual feels the same way.

2. *Keep your hands inside the vehicle at all times* doesn't just apply to rides at Disney World (a Heterosexual melting pot that we'll get to later); it also applies to Heterosexual Watching. In my years of Heterosexual Watching, I've learned that Heterosexuals do *not* like to be touched unexpectedly. Now that doesn't mean you can never touch a Heterosexual. Far from it. Kiss your Heterosexual grandma and hug your friendly Heterosexual tennis partner, but only do such touching if it's mutually agreed upon. Basically, what I'm saying is, no matter how many acai berry martinis you've had and no matter how nice your Heterosexual friend Mike has always been to you, never stick your hand inside his shirt, no matter how experienced a Heterosexual Watcher you may be, and no matter how well-toned Mike's chest has been looking lately.

3. If you see a Heterosexual, do not immediately point at him/her, as the Heterosexual will automatically assume that you're (A) a creep to be actively avoided, (B) a terrorist, or (C) a paparazzi photographer who is going to take a *really* unflattering picture of her at Chipotle and force her to explain why she was eating a burrito at 10 a.m. in the first place (if the Heterosexual is, say, Demi Lovato).*

Those are the rules. Other than that, remember to enjoy yourself and have a good time. Heterosexual Watching is a wonderful way to connect with a lovely species that is literally everywhere you go. Pay close attention, and maybe, just maybe, you'll learn a little something. Oh, and if you happen to be that hot guy in the baby blue–striped tank top from Starbucks . . . hey, gurl!

*True story!

Staggering Statistics on Heterosexuals

I also feel compelled to share with you some *very* important statistics to keep in mind about Heterosexuals and their lifestyle before beginning your journey as a Heterosexual Watcher.

 8 out of 10 Heterosexual Males claim to have played football in high school.

 4 out of 10 Heterosexual Males actually played football in high school.

 1 out of 10 Heterosexual Females is legitimately happy for Lea Michele.

 No Heterosexual Male has ever had an erotic dream about any of the cast members of *The Golden Girls*.

9 out of 10 Heterosexual Males know all the words to "Achy Breaky Heart" by Garth Brooks.

 1 out of 10 Heterosexual Males has watched an entire episode of *The Real Housewives of Beverly Hills*.

 1 out of 10 Heterosexual Males can pronounce the name *Fosse*.

 8 out of 10 Heterosexual Females have had sex with John Mayer.

 6 out of 10 Heterosexual Males will, at some point, date a girl named Amber and/or Nicole.

6 out of 10 Heterosexual Females have read *Eat, Pray, Love.*

 9 out of 10 Heterosexual Females have only read the "Eat" section of *Eat, Pray, Love.*

 8 out of 10 Heterosexual Males have slid across the floor in white socks, a white button-up, a pair of Hanes, and sunglasses à la Tom Cruise in *Risky Business* while home alone.

 10 out of 10 Heterosexual Females have dressed up as either a "sexy fairy" or a "sexy nurse" for Halloween.

 6 out of 10 Heterosexual Males have been the subject of an angry song by Taylor Swift.

9 out of 10 Heterosexual Females have issues related to a girl named Beth having much bigger boobs than they did in eighth grade.

 1 out of 10 Heterosexuals are willing to give Avril Lavigne a second chance.

 10 out of 10 Heterosexual Males own a solid-colored polo from the Gap.

 7 out of 10 Heterosexual Females still secretly hope Zack Morris is a real person and will one day propose to them. (P.S. I get it, honey!)

Let's move on and learn about the specific breeds within the Heterosexual community. Come along!

Chapter 1

Heterosexual Watching

THE HETEROSEXUAL KINGDOM IS ONE OF EXPANSIVE VARIETY. These wonderful creatures come in all different shapes, sizes, colors, and backgrounds. I've spotted so many different kinds of Heterosexuals in my life that I get excited just thinking about it—but I'm getting ahead of myself.

Unlike those really unappealing photos of food that are the same in every Chinese takeout place in every city in the history of the world, no two Heterosexuals are alike. Many Heterosexuals belong to very specific subsets and groups, such as Frat Boys, Married Couples, Hipsters, and Metrosexual Males.

Many other Heterosexuals belong to extremely rare subsets, such as hippies named Peter who live in vans in and around the greater Miami area; Asian Americans who lack computer skills; and the handful of people who think Cameron Diaz is a good actress (usually these same people also claim to have understood what the hell was going on in *Vanilla Sky*).

Heterosexual Watching requires that you fully understand what it is you're looking at when observing Heterosexuals in their natural habitat. Skilled Heterosexual Watchers will memorize these varied breeds so, when they're in the field, they do not have to consult the pages of this book.

In the event that you're not very good at memorizing because you didn't grow up doing community theater—or, in my case, even if you did, but you partied a little too hard during that blurry period of 2009 to 2011 when you lived in New York with that girl who was always doing drugs in your kitchen with the go-go dancers she met at nightclubs and have since then not been able to remember anything from your cousin Hal's birthday to where the hell you put your spare set of keys when you came in last night—you're more than welcome to bring along this guide anytime you're in the field.

However, it is vital to wait until after the Heterosexual has left the premises to consult the guide, since Heterosexuals tend to be fast creatures who come and go very quickly, and by looking down into the guide to determine whether the person is a Metrosexual or a Frat Boy, you might end up missing the spotting entirely. It is best to simply observe and take it in. Once you've fully watched the Heterosexual, then (and only then) should you consult the guide to determine what you've just seen.

Make sense? Great. Aw, really? Thanks. I'll bet you're really smart, too.

Breeds and Subsets of Heterosexuals

THE SINGLE WANNABE CARRIE BRADSHAW FEMALE

TOPOGRAPHY

A young woman, somewhere in age between the mid-20s and mid-30s, who moves to New York City in hopes of leading the Carrie Bradshaw lifestyle. She is usually astonished when she discovers just how much a pair of Jimmy Choos costs and how she feels after five cosmopolitans.

Q&A

Q. What do you do?

A. Currently I'm interning at a fashion magazine, but what I really want to do is write my own column, like Carrie Bradshaw.

This answer is code for: "I'd like to have a seemingly endless disposable income, obnoxious amounts of free time, and more shoes than I will have days in my lifetime."

HOW TO SPOT

She is usually clutching a copy of the September issue of *Vogue* (even if it's March). Also, look for colorful and patterned handbags that cost more than the four years she spent at BU, plus bold fashion choices that at first might resemble that of a homeless drag queen but under further inspection reveal themselves to be "high fashion"–chunky belts; unnecessarily high shoes; clothes or accessories with pictures of Audrey Hepburn on them; wrap dresses; vintage hats; clothing that looks like it was made for a child; clothing that actually *was* made for a child; a big smile that says, "I'm an ambitious girl with dreams, but I'm also a pretty easy lay"; and a big Starbucks coffee that says, "I'm a girl with a hangover, but I'm also a pretty easy lay."

BACKGROUND

Not really important; what is important is that she completely disregards where she came from, and never mentions her parents until season five when Miranda's mother dies and her laptop breaks in what is arguably the best episode of the series.

PHILOSOPHY AND BELIEFS

The Barneys co-op sale; Woody Allen movies about New York; saying things like, "New York is my playground"; "I would honestly die if I moved out of the West Village"; and "Brunch is my church."

DISPOSITION

Usually rather sunny. These Heterosexual Females have moved to a big city with infectiously positive dreams and hope. However, once they start their entry-level jobs at whatever fashion magazine they're working for, their dispositions grow wearier and wearier, until finally they lose their shit like Anne Hathaway's character in *The Devil Wears Prada*. Or, like Anne Hathaway herself probably did after those bizarre three hours of hosting the Oscars with James Franco.

AVERSIONS

The Gap; Times Square; being told, "You're such a Miranda."

MIGRATION PATTERN

Usually prefers migration to European cities where ridiculous fashion is socially acceptable and cigarettes are still considered chic instead of, y'know . . . cancerous.

HABITAT

This Heterosexual's habitat is usually rather modest, as most of her income goes into the aforementioned shoes and overpriced drinks served in chilled martini glasses. However, her sense of style makes up for her meager surroundings, and she can usually turn any old New York City walk-up apartment into something right out of your local Anthropologie window display. Likely because she usually works at your local Anthropologie.

TURN-ONS

Men with a sense of style; men with vacation homes; men who in any way could resemble Mr. Big; being compared to anyone from any French film ever; being mistaken for being French; pretending she knows how to read French when at a French restaurant; any sort of modern art museum that serves wine;

The Top 10 Things You Should Know about the Single Wannabe Carrie Bradshaw Female

1. She ate tasteless pasta for an entire month to be able to afford the shoes she's wearing; please compliment them.

2. She will never get onboard with Sloane Crosley, but will never suggest it is because she's jealous.

3. She actively avoids the term *old maid* or the card game of the same name.

4. When reacting to a friend's engagement, her enthusiasm is always fake, but she never acknowledges that.

5. She *loves* romantic comedies.

6. She *hates* romantic comedies.

7. Drunk texting is often a preferred method of correspondence. Such texts could include one to an ex-boyfriend: "I still can't believe your audacity," or to a female friend: "You're my gurl, Casey."

8. Never ask about her sister with the house in East Hampton, the CEO husband, and that amazing job in publishing. She'd rather not go there.

9. She secretly wishes it were actually President *Michelle* Obama.

10. Never, ever, ever even suggest that Sarah Jessica Parker and Carrie Bradshaw aren't the same person.

getting asked directions by tourists and giving them, even if she has absolutely no idea what she's talking about.

Sports bars; khaki pants; the subway; reality television that isn't on Bravo; New Jersey; carbs.

THE METROSEXUAL MALE

TOPOGRAPHY

Metrosexuals are an enigma of the species. On the surface, they're groomed, dressed, and displayed in a way that leads some to believe they're Homosexuals, but underneath the Kiehl's moisturizer, 2(x)ist underwear, and basic black Marc Jacobs polo is a very attractive and pleasantly scented Heterosexual.

Q&A

Q. Do people ever assume you're gay?
A. Of course. Every day.
Q. Are you OK with that?
A. I don't really see the comparison. Hey, I just made a goat cheese–and–fennel quiche. Would you like a bite?

HOW TO SPOT

Look for glamorous metropolitan male fashion (a lot of fitted shirts and pants with labels written in Italian), tailored suits that show off his toned body, as well as hair products that smell like Carson Kressley's house on Fire Island.

BACKGROUND

Metrosexuals come from all walks of life. They could be raised in the city, the country, or suburbia. The only requirement is that they get the hell out of wherever it is they're from, migrate to a major metropolitan area, and buy all the DKNY they can possibly afford.

PHILOSOPHY AND BELIEFS

Jon Hamm = God.

DISPOSITION

Metrosexuals carry themselves with an air of mystery. They know better than anyone that a brooding, serious demeanor goes really well with their charcoal Diesel mock turtleneck sweater that hasn't even come out in stores yet.

AVERSIONS

Baggy pants; body odor; Supercuts; Panda Express.

MIGRATION PATTERN

Metrosexuals love migrating to other big cities and can also enjoy sleepy New England towns, as long as they've brought a copy of anything by Fitzgerald and there's a bed-and-breakfast that's been profiled in the *New York Times* travel section for having a varied selection of aged bourbons.

Think you've spotted a Metrosexual? Here are some helpful questions to ask him.

Boxers or Briefs?
A Metrosexual would never wear boxers because he favors fitted pants and, to a Metrosexual, the only thing worse than scrunched-up boxer shorts in a pair of fitted slacks is when his DVR doesn't record *Top Chef*.

What kind of socks are you wearing?
Any Metrosexual will be able to answer this. Period. End of story.

How many products are in your hair right now?
Anything less than two and he's disqualified. Anything less than one and he's a wild animal.

How many times, in the past year, have you received some sort of spa treatment?
Anything less than four and he's disqualified. Bonus points if the Metrosexual can tell you what a paraffin dip is!

Thoughts on hair removal?
All Metrosexuals manscape. A Metrosexual thinks of back hair the same way I think of Debra Messing in dramatic roles. I know that a few exist, but that doesn't mean I ever have to see them.

Metrosexuals keep their homes spotless and orderly. If you enter a Metrosexual's den that is unkempt or dirty, you have walked into a crime scene, and you should immediately leave and call the police.

TURN-ONS

Girls with a distinctive fashion sense (Metrosexuals want their relationships to look like a photo spread in *Details* magazine); speakeasies; women who let them pick out the wine; cigars; modern art (even if they don't get it); *Mad Men*; anything made out of alligator skin; Victoria Beckham.

TURN-OFFS

Applebee's, country music, the state of Florida.

THE MARRIED COUPLE

TOPOGRAPHY

Two Heterosexuals, a male and female, who are married. These Heterosexual pairs are usually distinguished by rings on their left ring finger, patience in dealing with others, visible frustration, and the constant use of *we*.

Q&A

Recently, I sat down with a Heterosexual Married Couple named Frank and Alice who have been together for twenty years.

Me: Hi, Frank. Hi, Alice. Thanks for sitting down with me.

Frank: I'm happy to do it.

Alice: *I* am, too, Frank.

Frank: I know that, Alice. I was speaking for both of us.

Alice: Well, I'm perfectly capable of speaking for myself, thank you very much.

Frank: I know that, Alice.

Alice: And you didn't even mention me. You said, "*I'm* happy to do it." Not "*we.*"

Frank: The *we* was implied.

Alice: Then you should have said *we.*

Frank: And if you could speak for yourself then I shouldn't be the one to have to speak for you.

Alice: I was going to speak if you would just shut the fuck up for five seconds!

Me: So, what would you say is the hardest part of marriage?

Frank and Alice: **Communication.***

How to Spot

The Heterosexual Married Couple varies in appearance. Newly married couples maintain healthy, attractive appearances; however, once the marriage has reached roughly the 10-year mark, the couple's devotion to their appearance becomes less and less of a

----

*When Heterosexual Married Couples say this, what they really mean is, "Not ripping each other's throats out and stomping them into bloody pulps on a daily basis."

priority, eventually resulting in the wearing of sweatpants and the nightly television viewing of whatever is playing on TLC, which, let's be honest, is probably something about conjoined twins.

BACKGROUND

While background is not a major factor in the life of a Heterosexual Married Couple, their upbringing can sometimes come into play when they're fighting. Key phrases, such as "You sound just like your father" and "You're turning into your mother" can end a disagreement between a Married Couple faster than whatever began it, which, it should be noted, is *always* the Heterosexual Male's fault.

PHILOSOPHY AND BELIEFS

Many Married Couples include two people with extremely different views and beliefs. It took my own mother something like 15 years to tell my father that she was a closet Democrat and that she hates baby back ribs (two things that, as a rule, go hand in hand).

DISPOSITION

Married Couples can go from happy to not happy in a matter of seconds. A couple might be having a great day, but then the male might say something stupid about Claudia, the female's best friend, and all hell breaks loose. Married Couples must be able to say, "I'm sorry. I'm stupid. I was wrong. You're nothing like Satan, and neither is Claudia."

AVERSIONS

Infidelity. The biggest threat to a Married Couple is that woman who works in the man's office, who is always wearing those low-cut blouses that are three sizes too small and who smells like cigarettes mixed with Bath & Body Works, or that guy who works with the woman and who looks like a sexy Woody Harrelson and is always suggesting they go jogging together. These types of Heterosexuals are called home wreckers or Angelina Jolie.*

MIGRATION PATTERN

Married Couples love to travel, mainly because when you live with someone 24/7, you run out of things to talk about, so migration offers conversation starters like, "Hey! Look at that fountain!" and "I like the Chinese food at the mall back home *a lot* better than all this crap in Asia."

HABITAT

A Married Couple's habitat brings characteristics of the two Heterosexuals into one place. Usually the female's taste prevails over

---

*Angelina Jolie is an American actress and all around Weirdo with a capital W. When she broke up the beloved marriage of Brad Pitt and Saint Jennifer Aniston, she not only wrecked a home, but she divided a country. Those of us who never had that big of a problem with Angelina Jolie were forced to look at her as more than a nut job who made out with her brother when she won an Academy Award, and instead see her for who she really is: the woman who destroyed Rachel from *Friends'* life.

the male's, and his golf trophy from eight years ago is forced into a room called the Man Cave.*

When he does the dishes and she pretends to enjoy *The Expendables 2*.

TURN-OFFS
When their DVR forgets to record whatever Bravo reality show they're most into—usually *Top Chef*.

THE HIPSTER

TOPOGRAPHY
A Hipster is a Heterosexual Male or Female who rebels against popular culture and favors styles, tastes, and interests that are of the utmost hipness.

---

*The Man Cave is a designated room in a Married Couple's home where the male is allowed to keep all the things the female cannot abide, such as posters from Quentin Tarantino movies, video game systems, and a stained futon left over from the male's college dorm room that he cannot bear to part with because of the "memories" (a.k.a. that three-way he had with his girlfriend and Stacey, the chemistry major who lived next door and who always got naked anytime she was drunk or it was a weekday or a weekend).

Q. Are you a Hipster?

A. No. I'm an individual. One of a kind.

Q. Where did you get your shirt?

A. Urban Outfitters. Why?

How to Spot

Hipsters have one of the most distinctive looks among Heterosexuals. Hipsters favor skinny jeans, vintage shirts, colorful sneakers, thick-rimmed glasses, boots, "ironic" facial hair, and an attitude that says, "I don't care how bad I smell. Wanna read my zine?" If you're walking down the street and you see someone who looks like he's in a 1980s workout video; looks homeless but has an iPhone; or looks like he's stepped out of colonial times, you've most likely spotted a Hipster. If it's the latter, you might have just spotted an Amish person, in which case I have no suggestions on how to approach him, as my knowledge of Amish culture is limited to *For Richer or Poorer*, starring Tim Allen and Kirstie Alley.

Background

Hipsters often come from very wealthy backgrounds, but have chosen old clothes, dirty hair, and musky body odor as their ultimate form of rebellion against their type-A parents. Or they're European.

Philosophy and Beliefs

Hipsters *love* having a cause. Causes include gay marriage; the environment; Darfur; AIDS; hungry children; the homeless;

Recently, I sat down with the Heterosexual Hipster who works at my local coffee shop. His name is Zane, and he looks like a cleaner Tilda Swinton. Here is a direct transcript of our interview on the Heterosexual lifestyle and when he first "knew."

Me: Hi, Zane.

Zane: Good morning. What can I get ya?

Me: Can I get a nonfat iced latte with a triple shot?

Zane: Sure. Anything else?

Me: Hmm. Those scones look good.

Zane: They're delicious. The banana-nut is my favorite. And they're gluten-free!

Me: I'm good. Hey, are you a Heterosexual?

Zane: Um. Yeah.

Me: Fascinating. How long have you been one?

Zane: Um. My whole life, I guess.

Me: *Really*? How old are you?

Zane: 22.

Me: And you're telling me you've known you were Heterosexual for 22 years?

Me: When did you first know?

Zane: Yeah. I guess so. Your total is $2.15.

Me: That you're a Heterosexual.

Zane: Know what?

Me: Are you happy being a Heterosexual? How much did you say?

Zane: There really wasn't a specific moment.

Me: Do you have a girlfriend?

Zane: $2.15. Yeah, I'm happy.

Me: What's her name?

Zane: Yeah. Why?

Me: And is *she* a Heterosexual?

Zane: Katie.

Zane stares at me blankly until I go away.

P.S. Just in case you were dying to know, I did end up getting the banana-nut scone, and he was right—it *was* delicious.

the war; or Arcade Fire going too mainstream. Hipsters are also extremely vocal against gentrification in the areas where they are responsible for said gentrification.

DISPOSITION

A too-cool-for-school vibe, but they'd never use that term, or even the word *cool*, because they're too cool even for that.

AVERSIONS

Anything embraced by the masses, including *American Idol*, *The Bachelor*, Katy Perry, Russell Brand after he married Katy Perry, anything on CBS.

MIGRATION PATTERN

Hipsters love migrating to cities such as Portland, Seattle, and Austin. Also, anywhere with a used record store and a coffee shop run by people who don't make eye contact with you.

HABITAT

Hipsters usually live in ghettoized areas that cater to their Hipster way of life. In these habitats, you will find boutiques selling clothes made of organic cotton; lots of kale; gift shops that sell nothing but handmade soap; bars that serve Pabst Blue Ribbon; and a population where 40 percent of both the men and women look just like Michael Cera.

Food trucks; gelato; espresso; old-fashioned soda made with cane sugar; not having cable; talking about not having cable; knit caps; vests; naming their wireless networks after characters from *Twin Peaks*; claiming they were one of the first people to join Instagram; plaid; girls who look like Natalie Portman in *V for Vendetta*; boys who look like Daniel Day-Lewis in pretty much anything; paisley prints; irony.

Bank of America; acting like their parents; shopping malls; Julia Roberts movies; processed food; children; the book *Tuesdays with Morrie*; country music; and saying, "cool beans."

THE FRAT BOY

The term *Frat Boy* refers to men belonging to a fraternity, a college-based social group that works as a social members-only club, and puts young men in one house full of beer and unacknowledged homoerotic tension. Fraternities have all sorts of secret rules and activities, and one cannot simply join, but must earn admittance through humiliating activities that include anything from streaking across campus to getting paddled on the butt with a big wooden stick. Again, it's worth stressing that this is a *Heterosexual* activity. The Frat Boy is a male who is either currently in one of these fraternities or is an alum of a fraternity who hasn't been able to get over his glory days or get a job.

How to Spot

Frat Boys favor comfort over style: hats worn backward; expensive watches; boxer shorts with Homer Simpson's face printed on the butt; baggy pants; and T-shirts from places like American Eagle and Hollister. Nine times out of 10, a Frat Boy is wearing at least one article of clothing with a team number printed on it for absolutely no reason whatsoever. In some cases, Frat Boys who are no longer in college and are forced to join the real world will throw on a suit and tie for the daily grind. But you'd better believe that the Green Bay Packers T-shirt he wore all weekend without washing is getting a third act the minute he gets home.

Background

A Frat Boy can come from anywhere, but once he joins a fraternity, it will completely change his life for better and worse. The better being making lifelong friends, and the worse being liver failure and flunking out of Notre Dame all before his second semester of sophomore year.

Philosophy and Beliefs

Beer.

Disposition

Unbearably "fun."

The Most Frequently Asked Questions about Frat Boys

Q. What is a frat house?
A. A frat house is a structure (usually a beautiful old house) where fraternity brothers live together while attending college and beating *Guinness Book of World Records* statistics on the most tequila consumed by one human being, and avoiding the act of cleaning and/or studying.

Q. What does a frat house smell like?
A. A frat house is an extremely masculine environment, so expect extremely masculine smells, and if you're still confused as to what that means, open your dirty clothes hamper, dig all the way to the bottom while holding your nose, get as deep into the hamper as possible, then inhale the musky aroma, and you've pretty much smelled the inside of a frat house.

Q. So just what does the inside of a frat house look like?
A. Full disclosure: The closest thing to a frat house I've ever been in was the house where all the male dancers lived at the arts conservatory I went to for college, and not only did it smell of beautiful lavender candles, but it also looked like the inside of Nathan Lane's suitcase. Traditionally, a frat house will be decorated with hypermasculine décor, such as empty beer bottles displayed in rows atop cabinets and other flat surfaces; large poster images of women in swimsuits; *Family Guy* memorabilia; and any sort of signage that declares it to be Miller Time.*

*Miller Time is a designated hour in Heterosexual culture that can happen basically whenever someone declares it to be so. Once it is declared, everyone is expected to drink a Miller beer, no matter what time of day it is.

Aversions

Smart cars; anything considered "cute."

Migration Pattern

See Spring Break (page 142).

Habitat

Enter at your own risk. You know how when you leave dirty socks in your backpack for a few days, and then suddenly it's the weekend and you're like, "I'll wait until Monday to bring in my bag," and then Monday comes and your car smells like Mickey Rourke after a jog through the desert? That's how a Frat Boy's habitat will most likely smell.

Turn-Ons

Naked women; keg stands;* beer; TV shows about monster trucks; epic Saturday nights; nicknaming one's penis something like the General or Captain Corona; porn; movies in which cars

---

*A keg stand is when a Heterosexual positions himself upside down atop a keg of cold beer. The object of a keg stand is to chug beer from the keg's spout until one falls off or passes out. I have done a keg stand *once* in my entire life, and it was at a party in someone's backyard. There were tons of Heterosexuals there, but when I did this alleged keg stand, I counterbalanced it by the fact that I happened to be wearing a costume from the local community theater's production of *Cats* (long story). No joke. You're reading the words of a man who's done a keg stand in a lycra body suit and cat ears meant for a musical theater character named Rum Tum Tugger.

explode; movies in which entire cities explode; movies in which people explode; and did I already mention beer?

Sushi; documentaries; *The New Yorker*; wearing a shirt; blogs about performance art; this book.

THE OUTSPOKEN LIBERAL

TOPOGRAPHY

Many Heterosexuals are outspoken supporters of liberal causes and politics. Generally, these Heterosexuals are savvy urbanites who have donated at least $50 to National Public Radio within the past six months and carry around a *Fresh Air with Terry Gross* tote bag to prove it.

HOW TO SPOT

Outspoken Liberal Heterosexuals usually look just like everyone else, except maybe slightly more stylish, considering their frequent exposure to gay friends.

BACKGROUND

The greatest thing about being an Outspoken Liberal is that you can be from anywhere you want to be. However, those from Georgia or Louisiana should be prepared for skepticism.

Basically anything that Rush Limbaugh would consider "un-American."

Good listeners, or at least they're good at positioning their very trendy glasses on the tip of the nose and making an expression that looks like they're listening.

Close-mindedness; inequality; Jeff Foxworthy.

Open-minded places, such as Vermont, San Francisco, and the literary theory section at Barnes & Noble.

Aesthetically pleasing and unique spaces, including lofts, old buildings converted into houses, and homes with colorful histories and enlightening stories the Outspoken Liberal can share at dinner parties (i.e., "You know, this was Buster Keaton's house for like two months before he drank himself to death").

Activism; singer-songwriters; film festivals; feminist poetry; pictures of Michelle Obama gardening; Internet-based comedians; Dylan Thomas quotes as Facebook statuses; dogs named after

The Top 10 Things the Outspoken Liberal Heterosexual Says

1. "If he gets elected, I'm moving to Canada."

2. "I need a new pair of Tom's."

3. "I had a sex dream about Jon Stewart last night. Again."

4. "John Lennon made some really good points."

5. "I voted for Hillary the first time, but I love Barack!"

6. "The wireless password is YesWeCan. All one word."

7. "I'm not gay, but if I were, I'd be *all* over Rachel Maddow."

8. "That was back when I was still eating at Chick-fil-A."

9. "It's a shame, because I actually used to like Clint Eastwood."

10. "I actually *hope* my son is gay."

any character in *To Kill a Mockingbird*; NBC Thursday night comedies; Showtime; iPads; iPhones; iTV; iMac; iCed coffee (see what I did there?); and Aaron Sorkin.

TURN-OFFS

Anyone with the name *Bush* (and that includes the beans); country clubs; racism; jokes about fat people (unless they're Republican congressmen, then bombs away); deep-fried anything; PC computers; Westboro Baptist Church; corn dogs.

THE OUTSPOKEN CONSERVATIVE

TOPOGRAPHY

The Outspoken Conservative Heterosexual is a male or female who is basically the opposite of the Outspoken Liberal. He/she leans to the right on political and social issues. These Heterosexuals put "traditional values" before all else, and yet they still find Bristol Palin endearing.

HOW TO SPOT

The Outspoken Conservative comes in many different shapes, sizes, and colors. However, the majority are Caucasian people who love anything with an American flag printed on it.

BACKGROUND

Outspoken Conservatives are usually raised by other Outspoken

Conservatives, and often come from places where people wear hats sized by the gallon.

PHILOSOPHY AND BELIEFS
A deep love for "traditional American values" and ground beef.

DISPOSITION
Vitriolic patriotic chic.

AVERSIONS
People named José; Kathy Griffin; anyone who has ever been a judge on *Project Runway*; the "liberal media"; JCPenney; the word *choreography*; mosques; men who refer to Dame Judi Dench as "my diva"; the phrase *Happy Holidays*.

MIGRATION PATTERN
The nearest Cracker Barrel.*

HABITAT
Outspoken Conservative Heterosexuals can be found all over; however, many have chosen states such as Alabama, Georgia,

---

*Cracker Barrel is a restaurant chain specializing in the kind of food your grandma would have made. It's known for its comfortable rocking chairs on the front porch, its liberal use of gravy, and the gift shops you must walk through in order to be seated. These gift shops sell everything you could ever need if you're a 50-something-born-again Christian woman who is in the market for an old-fashioned chess set or an *Andy Griffith Show* puzzle.

The Top 10 Things the Outspoken Conservative Heterosexual Says

1. "If he gets elected, I'm moving to Canada."

2. "Let's keep Christ in Christmas."

3. "Even I didn't have the heart to vote for Palin."

4. "Is it OK to like the Dixie Chicks again yet?"

5. "Communism!!!"

6. "Socialism!!!"

7. "I once knew a Jewish guy in college."

8. "More like Michael *Bore*."

9. [Shouting in public as if at a sports game, but not actually at a sports game] "USA! USA! USA!"

10. "Does that come with fries?"

Florida, and Tennessee to call home. Most flock to areas surrounding the Heterosexual shopping mecca known as Walmart.

TURN-ONS

Domestic beer; photos of women holding guns; Bill O'Reilly; organizing protests against effeminate cartoon characters; beauty pageants; buying in bulk; supporting their country; when people thank Jesus after winning an Oscar or the Super Bowl or a Golden Globe; any chance they can remind you how much they support the troops.

TURN-OFFS

The West Coast; hippies; Jane Fonda; gay marriage; holistic medicine; the Tony Awards; single-parent homes; tarot cards; food they cannot pronounce; me.

THE BEST-FRIEND-TO-THE-GAYS

TOPOGRAPHY

This Heterosexual Female surrounds herself with gay men. Why? Because she likes to have a good time. She is usually single, employed, and eager to do anything her gay best friend Chad says. Through Chad, she will discover Cher's early cover songs, how to infuse her own tequila, and why it's not OK to wear flip-flops in a gay bar (or anywhere for that matter).

How to Spot

She dresses a little flashy, in an attempt to compete with the gay men she is surrounded by. She can be found sporting bold colors, excessive makeup, and sometimes even sequins on a Monday. If she knows one thing, it's that you've got to get up extremely early to outdress a drag queen.

Background

Her parents are still married; that's why her standards have remained so high when dating. She worries that she'll never find a love as strong as her own parents', so until that day comes, she'll be watching early Diane Keaton movies with Chad every night. (By the way, am I the only person who's dying to be friends with Chad? He sounds great.)

Philosophy and Beliefs

The perfect friend and the perfect person to sing "Summer Lovin'" from *Grease* with at karaoke.

Disposition

When she gets drunk, her mood changes from a fun, bubbly time to the biggest headache in Chad's life. It will become Chad's responsibility to drag her out of the bar, kicking and screaming, and force her into a cab, in which she will most likely vomit before asking Chad, through heavy tears, if he thinks he will ever sleep with her, even just once.

The Top 10 Things the Best-Friend-to-the-Gays Wants to Hear

1. "Are you Chad's younger sister?"

2. "You look like a Disney heroine."

3. "I *love* your shoes!" (when said by a drag queen)

4. "I'm gay, but if I were going to hook up with a girl, it would *so* be you!"

5. "We should *totally* be Mary Kate and Ashley Olsen for Halloween!" (when said by Chad)

6. "You should seriously have your own reality show."

7. "You are a diva!"

8. "I wish I had the courage to have your bangs."

9. "You should sing live somewhere besides karaoke."

10. "I love you because you tell it like it is!"

AVERSIONS

Other females who threaten her relationship with Chad.

MIGRATION PATTERN

Wherever Chad brings her.

HABITAT

You guessed it. With Chad.

TURN-ONS

Shirtless photos of Matt Bomer, calling herself Chad's "Grace," an eclectic taste in music, being compared to Scarlett Johannson, and Chad.

TURN-OFFS

Chad's new boyfriend, Jake.

There are also numerous other smaller groups within the Heterosexual community, including the following:

THE ADORKABLE HETEROSEXUAL GIRL

Thanks in part to quirky celebrities like Zooey Deschanel, Heterosexuals have coined the term *adorkable*. I know what you're thinking: what an obnoxious word. And you know what? You're absolutely, 100 percent right. However, this spotter's guide wouldn't be complete without mentioning this adorably nerdy girl who decks herself out in clothes her mom wore in high school, the girl who can play '90s Nickelodeon theme songs on her ukulele, and the girl who carries a Hello Kitty lunch box for a purse.

THE 50-AND-FABULOUS HETEROSEXUAL FEMALE

This Heterosexual Female is 50-something, and, thanks in part to extremely vocal celebrities like Jamie Lee Curtis, has vowed to be fabulous in her middle age. Furthermore, this Heterosexual Female makes it her mission to let literally everyone know about this by constantly shouting, "I'm 50 and fabulous!" any time she's had even half a glass of chardonnay.

The Top 10 Things That the 50-and-Fabulous Likes

1. Fitting into her daughter's clothes.

2. Talking about how she can fit into her daughter's clothes.

3. Totally age-inappropriate shirtless photos of Patrick Schwarzenegger.

4. Full-body Spanx.

5. Josh Groban.

6. Michael Bublé.

7. Referencing Helen Mirren's impressive beach body any chance she gets.

8. *Fifty Shades of Grey*.

9. Flirting with waiters who may or may not be the same age as her son.

10. Saint Lane Bryant.

THE MIDLIFE CRISIS MALE

A similar case to the 50-and-Fabulous Female, but drastically different in approach. The Midlife Crisis Male* has had a similar awakening to live his middle age to the fullest; however, this springs from the desire to have sex with women in their 20s and drive a sports car, as opposed to feeling fabulous. The Midlife Crisis Male will often leave his wife for a younger woman, will attempt to grow a ponytail, and, for a brief period, will shorten his name to something like Chet.

THE SASSY BLACK LADY

The Sassy Black Lady can fit in anywhere among the Heterosexual culture and beyond. Church? Certainly! Football games? Sure. Gay bars? Definitely. Straight bars? Yes. Reality television? It's a match made in heaven.

---

*The ultimate Midlife Crisis Male is Ryan O'Neal. Once a handsome movie star, now a whacky old man who shows up on talk shows every once in a while to seem drunk and say something crazy. Ryan O'Neal slipped so far into the Midlife Crisis Male lifestyle that he tried to pick up his estranged daughter after not recognizing her at his girlfriend's funeral. *Classy*.

My Top Five Favorite Sassy Black Heterosexual Ladies

1. **Nene Leakes:** This Sassy Black Lady got famous for being a Real Housewife, by which I mean throwing drinks in people's faces and saying things like, "I got yo number, hussy!"

2. **Phylicia Rashad:** an American institution since 1952.

3. **Madea:** Sure, she's just Tyler Perry in drag, but she's still fantastic. And Tyler Perry is a Heterosexual. Right?

4. **Karen:** A lady who lives in my building and always greets me in the elevator by saying, "Oh, hey, sugar pie honey sweet baby darlin'." She really *gets* me.

5. **Star Jones:** By far one of the craziest people in the United States and hands down my favorite African-American former talk show personality who got fired after having an insanely public marriage to what turned out to be a gay man, and then had gastric-bypass surgery.

THE I'M-NOT-GAY-BUT-I-MADE-OUT-WITH-A-GIRL-IN-COLLEGE HETEROSEXUAL FEMALE

This Heterosexual Female reached her peak in college and is still struggling to regain that same enthusiasm, happiness, and secure social circle that suited her so well during her long-gone days at Florida State. After one too many appletinis, this Heterosexual Female always tells the story that once, during freshmen year, she got really drunk at the White Trash Party and ended up making out with Meagan Taylor. She doesn't know it, but this is the last time she was happy.

JACK NICHOLSON

There's only one, but it needed to be said.

THE CAT LADY

The Cat Lady is a long-standing subgroup of the Heterosexual population. This female has a stable job, a Time Warner Cable subscription, at least two cats, and one or all of the *Twilight* books on her nightstand at all times. While this female has some semblance of a social life and an impressively high score on online Monopoly, she much prefers the comforts of a DVR-ed episode of *Castle* to the ever-grueling world of dating, relationships, or leaving the house. The Heterosexual Cat Lady is my spirit animal.

THE GAMER

This Heterosexual Male spends the majority of his time in sweatpants, playing video games. Oftentimes he's self-employed or works from home as a telemarketer, blogger, or as the actor Seth Rogen. Girlfriends are usually nonexistent, fictional, or incredibly frustrated.

THE TEEN MOM

With the assistance of surging hormones and keys to her family's lake house, this Heterosexual Female accidentally becomes pregnant. This phenomenon has been heavily documented on the MTV series *Teen Mom*, where real-life Teen Moms are made famous for having sex without a condom, then screaming at their mom for not buying more toilet paper. Teen Moms are the seagulls of Heterosexuals, in that they're quite common and often migrate to Florida.

THE ELDERLY HETEROSEXUAL

Your grandparents are likely Elderly Heterosexuals, so you probably know this is a culture of people with very old-fashioned sensibilities and opinions. Sure, they might say something a little racist from time to time, but it's best to over-look it and enjoy the short time you have left to spend with them. These Heterosexuals tend to be extremely skilled at baking pies from scratch, not claiming their own farts, and constantly asking the same question: "Why isn't Milton Berle around anymore?" For more extensive research on the Elderly Heterosexual, watch an episode of *The Golden Girls* or just follow Betty White on Twitter.

Now that you understand the prevalent breeds within the Heterosexual kingdom, you are one step closer to being a skilled Heterosexual Watcher. Remember: Try to memorize these breeds so you don't have to consult the guide while you're out in the field, and if you have any questions, just give me a call.

Chapter 2

Heterosexual Habitats

IN THIS CHAPTER, I'M GOING TO DISCUSS HETEROSEXUAL HABITATS. When it comes to habitat, every Heterosexual is as different as each member of the Jackson family. However, now that I'm thinking about it, everyone in the Jackson family is pretty similar to everyone else in the Jackson family, by which I obviously mean *bat shit crazy*.

Heterosexuals tend to gravitate toward comfort more than the experimental style found among other species, with some rare exceptions that I will discuss below.

I grew up in a lovely Heterosexual home that included many staples that will help you get a sense of what you're likely to find in a Heterosexual Habitat:

- An enormous portrait photograph of an eight-year-old me made to look like a photograph from the twenties. (Heterosexuals *love* making old-fashioned-looking family photos.)

- A shotgun stored under my parents' bed.

- A plaid sofa with matching pillows.

- A leather recliner. (Heterosexual Males think of leather recliners the same way I think of coming home and putting a Lily Tomlin comedy album on my record player and pretending I'm her for a solid two hours, by which I mean it relaxes them.)

- Every *Southern Living* cookbook that's been published since 1975.

- Three copies of the Bible that various family members gave to me when I was born, but inside of which I wrote my name over and over until I learned to write other basic kid words like *pee pee* and *Liza*.

- Catalogues from places like *Eddie Bauer*, *J. Crew*, and *Cigar of the Month Club*.

- Female hygiene products under every sink in the house.*

- A liquor cabinet that would always remain stocked until I turned 17 and realized I lived somewhere with a liquor cabinet that always remained stocked.

This is just an example of one Heterosexual home. Not all Heterosexual Habitats have the aforementioned things, except for plaid sofas. *Every* Heterosexual owns a plaid sofa. There are a handful of other things you can find in almost every Heterosexual home as well.

---

*The day that a pack of female hygiene products arrived in the bathroom my older sister and I shared, I was *extremely* confused, but didn't want to ask because I sensed I wasn't supposed to. Instead, I opened a pack of women's pads and wore one inside my briefs for an entire day of school just to see how it felt. And my family was surprised when I told them I was gay.

The Top 10 Things That Are Most Commonly Found in the Home of a Heterosexual

1. A zip-up Snuggie with the label L.L. Bean or Patagonia.

2. Clogs (any sort of clog, but usually one made by Clarks).

3. Coupons for Domino's Pizza stuck to the refrigerator with a magnet in the shape of West Virginia.

4. Two or more products made by Old Spice.

5. *Remember the Titans* on DVD.

6. One of those electronic, taxidermied fish that sings "Take Me to the Water" when you push the red button.

7. Country Apple–scented candles.

8. A CD tower containing Alanis Morissette's album *Jagged Little Pill* that hasn't been touched since 1999, but that no one has thought to get rid of.

9. Any sort of cowboy hat or variation thereof.

10. A weathered copy of *The Joy of Cooking* on the same shelf as Rachael Ray's *30-Minute Meals*.

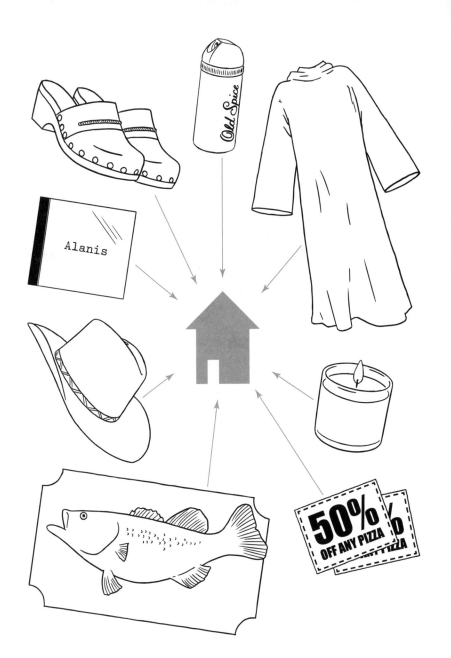

The Habitats

It's highly likely that you'll find at least one of those items in any of the popular Heterosexual Habitats outlined below. These are the most common habitats of the Heterosexual.

Major Metropolitan Areas

Many Heterosexuals can be found in major metropolitan areas, usually in a one-bedroom apartment or duplex. These Heterosexuals typically vote Democratic, have tried Indonesian food at least once, claim to have seen all of Wes Anderson's movies, and personally know a bare minimum of three aspiring graphic novelists. These Heterosexuals procreate less frequently than others of their species, based solely on the fact that their apartments are usually a maximum of 500 square feet. Heterosexual archetypes like the Outspoken Liberal (page 51), the Single Wannabe Carrie Bradshaw Female (page 31), and the Metrosexual (page 35) can be found in these environments.

The Golf Course Subdivision

An elite group of very attractive, purebred Heterosexuals reside in golf course subdivisions (sprawling green landmasses Heterosexuals flock to for a quiet, never-ending escapade called golf,* which utilizes sticks, balls, and high-priced polo shirts). These golf course subdivisions are their own communities of manicured

---

*See Golf (page 92).

lawns, enormous SUVs, and Junior Service Leagues—and some of them even allow black people nowadays! Heterosexual archetypes like Outspoken Conservatives (page 54) and Married Couples (page 38) can be found in these environments.

Rural Areas

Many Heterosexuals prefer the quiet comfort of nature and seclusion. Far from city life, these Heterosexuals build a habitat among the silent splendor of the great outdoors (the place, not the movie with John Candy and Annette Bening*). These Heterosexuals reside in a variety of nests, including cabins, AirStream trailers, and double-wides. They are most identifiable by their dirty coats and broad collections of belt buckles and/or bolos. Pretty much any Heterosexual archetype can be found in these places—except for the Metrosexual. If there's one thing Metrosexuals avoid it is double-wides—as well as Willie Nelson music and Kraft Macaroni & Cheese.

Suburbia

Located just outside a large city, these suburban neighborhoods are for working-class Heterosexual families interested in strip malls, good schools, T.J. Maxx clearance sales, day care, and reliable places to rent those inflatable play units for children's birthday parties. These communities were portrayed perfectly on

---

*Two actors popular with Heterosexuals, but neither popular enough to win Academy Awards.

the hit TV series *Desperate Housewives* (minus the excessive murder, adultery, and Felicity Huffman*). Heterosexual archetypes such as the Married Couple (page 38) *love* suburbia.

These next locales are specific places and are slightly less common as Heterosexual Habitats than the ones mentioned above, but are still popular enough to warrant discussion.

Seattle

This is a habitat many Heterosexuals call home. Besides having the highest suicide rate of any American city, Seattle has provided the world with such Heterosexual favorites as Starbucks, Pearl Jam, and iconic Heterosexual music artist Kenny G. If you get stuck in a conversation with Heterosexuals from Seattle, chances are they *love* to talk about how happy they are to live there, so stick with that.

Nashville

Known for its country music scene, this Heterosexual mecca is home to some of the world's biggest country music superstars. Heterosexual stars like Martina McBride, Keith Urban, and Carrie Underwood call this Southern city home. For me, Nashville stands out because not only does Keith Urban live there, but so does his wife, Nicole Kidman! One time my mom's friend Sharon *met* Nicole Kidman in the bathroom of a Cracker Barrel while visiting Tennessee, and if that's not a reason to live there, then I don't know what is.

---

*I do not endorse *any* of those three things.

The San Fernando Valley

Located just outside of Los Angeles, this area could arguably be included in the suburbia category, but I think it deserves its own mention. The San Fernando Valley is where Heterosexuals working in show business live, due to easy access to sizable houses, pretty lawns, and an abundance of drive-through food options.

Vermont

The most liberal of Outspoken Liberals (page 51) live in Vermont. It's the kind of place where lesbian-used bookstores that specialize in mysteries written in the 1970s are more common than corporate-owned grocery stores. Heterosexuals living in Vermont have names like Jade, Zane, and Peaceflower Jones.

Obviously, these aren't the only places you'll find Heterosexuals. That's the beauty of Heterosexuals—they're everywhere. Maybe you know some great Heterosexual Habitats you think I might have forgotten. If so, maybe you should stop being so critical and turn to the next page so I can teach you about the Heterosexual lifestyle. See what I did there? That's called a transition. It's also called throwing shade!*

---

*What is shade? First of all, this is not a Heterosexual term; in fact, it is far from it. Shade describes the tell-it-like-it-is attitude of gay men, drag queens, and a handful of Sassy Black Ladies (page 63). For example, look over at that very gay cashier in the store you're standing in and watch as he rolls his eyes and judgmentally glares at that woman who's been staring at blouses in the clearance section for the past two hours. That is shade.

Chapter 3

The Heterosexual Lifestyle

THE HETEROSEXUAL LIFESTYLE MIGHT SURPRISE SOME OF YOU. For others, it might be exactly what you expected. If you're part of the latter group, please go along with this because the rest of the class (by the way, I've started thinking of this as a class and I'm the teacher, but a nice teacher, like the cute, young guy teacher on *Glee*, not Jane Lynch and her startlingly broad shoulders) isn't as worldly as you.

Now that you've learned about so many breeds of Heterosexuals, you might be overwhelmed by exactly how to spot one of them. Fear not. If you know what key physical traits to look for, spotting a Heterosexual can be as easy as tying your shoes—unless you don't have hands, in which case, how did you pick up this book and turn to this page to begin with? You, dear reader, are a true survivor.

How to Spot a Heterosexual Male

This is clearly a Heterosexual Male. How can I tell? Because I'm *very* smart. Also because I have studied the Heterosexual Male so closely that I have received more restraining orders than Michael Lohan. The Heterosexual Male gives himself away through many distinguishing features that you, too, can spot in the Heterosexuals around you.

Facial Hair

This Heterosexual hasn't shaved in at least four days, and has no intention of doing so anytime soon. See the way it grows in full across his chin and upper lip? It's not because he's going for the scruffy international look that I've been trying to master since 2009; it's because this Heterosexual spends too much time playing World of Warcraft, and because his girlfriend has always had a thing for truckers.

Jeans

Jeans are almost always the perfect indicator. The typical Heterosexual Male prefers the comfort of a loose pair of jeans, usually a straight-leg or "carpenter-style" cut, with the added mind-set of the more pockets the better. Oftentimes, these pockets feature an embroidered pattern or design on the back that looks like something Prince would have changed his name to in the mid-1990s.

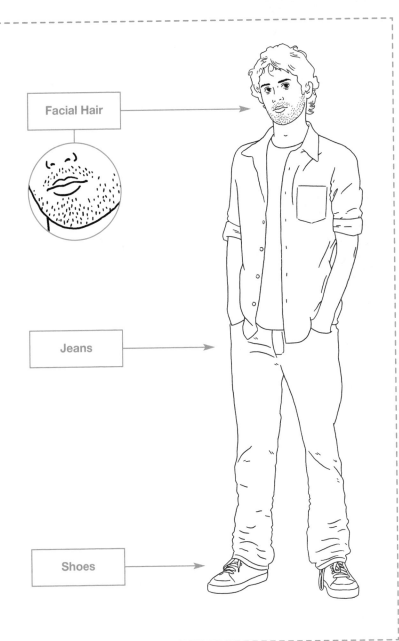

Facial Hair

Jeans

Shoes

Boxers or Briefs

When spotting any male in a pair of boxer shorts, you can pretty much assume that he is a Heterosexual. Personally, I haven't worn a pair of pants loose enough to wear with boxers since I was at least 12 or 13. That said, I also have a Kelly Ripa tank top hanging in my closet.

The *Ne Plus Ultra* Signifier: Shoes

Shoes are the clearest marker of the Heterosexual. The Heterosexual Male loves a comfortable shoe above all else. Back when I lived in New York, I could determine a hot guy's sexuality in a matter of seconds just by glancing down at his shoes on the subway. Robin's-egg blue Pumas with skinny jeans? *Not* a heterosexual. A pair of Reeboks that look so old they might have gone to elementary school with Cloris Leachman? Heterosexual!

Now, there is one exception that tosses all previously discussed rules and ideas out the window, by which I mean Europeans! European Males can really throw you for a loop when you're Heterosexual Watching. They are the juggernaut of all Heterosexual spotting, much like their cousins the Metrosexuals. The European fashion, coiffed hair, and extensive cultural taste might lead one to automatically assume that he's gayer than a *Flipping Out* marathon on Bravo, but with European Males you must look closer to determine whether or not you've spotted a Heterosexual. Here are some helpful questions to ask yourself while attempting to determine whether the man you've spotted is gay or merely European.

The Top 10 Ways to Tell If He's Gay or European

1. Does he speak with an accent?

2. Are you *sure* it's an accent and not the voice of someone trained to be a professional theater actor?

3. When you say *the Queen*, does he assume you're speaking about Queen Elizabeth or Olivia Newton-John?

4. Hold up a photo of Victoria Beckham and wait for his response. If he's European and straight, he'll say something like "She's a total 10, mate!" But if he's gay, he'll simply point at the photo and shout "*Diva!*"

5. What do his teeth look like? I'm not saying that *no* European man has good teeth, but I *am* saying that no gay man has bad teeth.

Gay

European

6. Turn on Beyoncé's "Love on Top" and see what happens to his shoulders. This will answer any and all questions you have, plus it's one of the best pop songs ever.

7. Look at the people he follows on Twitter. Keira Knightley? European. Kyra Sedgwick? Gay.

8. European men are still pissed off at Sarah Ferguson, the former Duchess of York, for attempting to sell stories about the Prince to tabloids. However, gay people simply get her confused with Wynonna Judd and will use this as an opportunity to make a jab at Wynonna's movie star sister, Ashley.

9. European men are still into capri pants, and gay men haven't gone near them since before Justin Bieber was born.

10. Ask him if he's seen Mary-Kate and Ashley Olsen's movie *Winning London*. If he's never heard of it, he's likely European. If he has seen it, he's most definitely gay and, on a sidenote, has extremely questionable taste.

Try to avoid topics such as *Downton Abbey*, Elton John, fitted V-neck T-shirts, comedian Graham Norton, and glasses designed by Oliver Peoples, as these discussions will merely leave you just as confused as you were to begin with.

How to Spot a Heterosexual Female

Spotting a Heterosexual Female can prove a bit more difficult than spotting the Heterosexual Male. While Heterosexual Males sport many unique accessories and articles of clothing that easily identify them as straight, the Heterosexual Female may be a bit more mysterious. Look to these key warning signs to help you in your spotting.

A Perfectly Messy Bun

What *is* a perfectly messy bun? It's when the Heterosexual Female gets her hair into just the right bun that appears effortlessly stylish and seemingly accidental. The sole intention of wearing a perfectly messy bun is to make both her friends and strangers see her and wonder, "Gosh, Lisa doesn't even have to *try* to look flawless." On average, a Heterosexual Female will spend upwards of an hour and 45 minutes perfecting this perfectly messy bun.

The Boyfriend Tee

This is a T-shirt that closely resembles or actually is the Heterosexual Female's boyfriend's T-shirt. Usually very soft from excess washing and oversized (unless the Heterosexual Female is partnered with a little person, in which case all bets are off and P.S. can I meet him?). The intention of the shirt is to let the world know that the Heterosexual Female has a boyfriend without her having to announce it everywhere she goes. Special

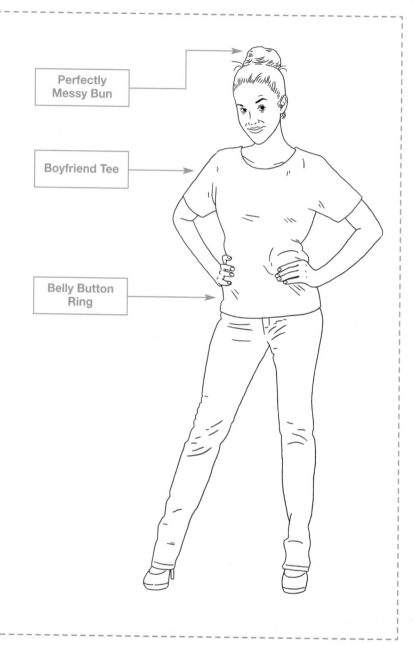

Perfectly
Messy Bun

Boyfriend Tee

Belly Button
Ring

points are given to boyfriend tees that feature the emblem of her boyfriend's alma mater. Someone, maybe not even the Heterosexual Female, maybe a gay man in his early 20s who has a great life and a lot to offer the world but just couldn't quite get it together enough to go on a date from the years of 2005 through 2010, but is really nice and hey, he wrote a book (doesn't that count for something?), might have, at one time in 2010, bought an old, worn-out T-shirt at a local thrift shop and wore it to coffee with friends and claimed it belonged to "Phillip from Hoboken" just to make himself feel a little less lonely. Hypothetically.

Belly Button Rings

Now, I'm not saying *all* Heterosexual Females have these, but a lot of them do. The belly button ring is found on a very specific kind of Heterosexual Female. To generalize, one who expects to show her midriff often enough to warrant stabbing a hole through her naval and decorating it with a cheap earring. Why do these Heterosexual Females do this? Who knows, but my theory is that it serves as a tracking device within the Heterosexual species, a calling card to let possible romantic candidates know "I'm proud of my tummy and I want to mate with you," without having to say that out loud.

Diet Coke

All Heterosexual Females prefer Diet Coke over any other soda option. Ordering a Diet Coke serves as a verbal mantra for the

Heterosexual Female that she is, in fact, doing her part to stay fit. Even though the words she uttered before this were *disco fries with extra gravy*.

Brunch

You can spot a Heterosexual Female at brunch by eavesdropping on her conversation with friends. Topics that will immediately reveal the female as Heterosexual include the cost of moisturizers, Isaac Mizrahi's fashion line at Target, how the female's boyfriend and/or husband doesn't appreciate Gayle King nearly enough, the books of Emily Griffin, guilt over how many Weight Watchers points are involved in ordering the pecan French toast, and declaring "I'm worth it" in regard to said French toast and the six mimosas she has just consumed.

Girls' Night and Boys' Night

Another easy way to spot Heterosexual Females is by observing them in a popular ritual known as a girls' night. A girls' night is a social practice among Heterosexual Females that isn't all that different than brunch, except that no one orders French toast and if they do it isn't my place to judge. These events are held on a designated night for them to gather together, let loose, drink cosmopolitans, and have a night just for the ladies. Customarily, they are held in high-end restaurants and bars, but in some cases they are held in unusual venues, such as nail salons, spas, and sex shops where Heterosexual Females purchase boxes of dried pasta in the shape of male genitalia and are given tutorials on how to give better blow jobs.

During a girls' night, Heterosexual Females discuss their careers, their hopes, and their dreams, but most often complain about the Heterosexual Males in their lives. Some experts say a girls' night is simply code for a "Can I talk about how bad my boyfriend's balls smell?!" night. This therapeutic practice of getting together with friends to get things off one's chest is frequently compared to traditional Native American powwows, Wiccan Sabbat rituals, or AA meetings, except, y'know, with booze.

These evenings tend to get rowdy and loud and are not meant for the inexperienced Heterosexual Watcher. You must enter these encounters on high alert, as there's a fair chance you'll end up seeing a grown woman cry over something that happened to her in high school or a mother of three confess that the only way she can have an orgasm is to watch Johnny Depp in *What's Eating Gilbert Grape*.*

Heterosexual Females aren't the only ones to have a special night like this; Heterosexual Males do it just as often as Females, however, with vastly different intentions and activities. This is called a boys' night.

Like a girls' night, a boys' night is a designated evening for Heterosexual Males to bond and cut loose. Heterosexual Males gather, usually in living rooms but sometimes in sports bars, around television sets broadcasting games such as football, basketball, and baseball. To fully understand a boys' night, you must first understand the sports around which these evenings are often planned.**

Football

Of all the sports out there, I probably understand this one the least, unless you count dog fighting as a sport, but if you do then put this book down and turn yourself into the police right now. I do *not* support dog fighting, and I don't have the time or the energy to try to explain football to someone who does. So *go*! Get out of here. Football is an extremely complex game in which two

---

*I had the same problem until I saw Brad Pitt in *Thelma and Louise*.

**I don't want to inflate grotesque stereotypes of gay people like myself knowing nothing about anything other than David Sedaris and glitter, but honestly, I have no gay friends who would rather watch sports than a rerun of *Toni Braxton: E! True Hollywood Story*.

teams compete to be in control of a strange-shaped ball made from the skin of a pig. Football players wear helmets, cleats, jerseys, and huge shoulder pads that surpass even the ones worn on such '80s television programs as *Dynasty* and *Designing Women*.

Baseball

If someone put a gun to my head and forced me to watch a sports game on TV, I'd (A) be *really* weirded out by the hostility and probably call 9-1-1 and (B) pick baseball. By default, baseball is my favorite sport, by which I mean it's the only sport I have ever watched with my dad and come close to understanding. It's pretty easy to comprehend; again, there are two teams (which seems to be a common theme with these sports) and again they are using a ball (another common theme), but this time the ball is smaller and not made of pigskin. However, I'm not sure what material is used in its place. Maybe it's like a pigeon's anal glands or something. In baseball, they introduce another prop, which is a bat. These bats are not to be confused with the ones that fly around at night and turn into Robert Pattinson; they are long, heavy shafts used to hit the ball into the air. Then the object of the game is to run to three different bases before the ball is thrown back to the catcher, a man covered in a long pad that looks like a massaging mattress pad from Brookstone and a helmet. When a player is able to pass all three bases before the ball gets back to the catcher, it is called a home run, an achievement that sends Heterosexual fans into the kind of crazy frenzy found at race-related riots and Katy Perry concerts.

Golf

This is *not* a team sport, which makes it a great afternoon hobby for wealthy Heterosexual men and unemployed lesbians. In this game, one uses the tiniest ball yet. It is definitely not made from the skin of an animal, but is instead made from a very hard plastic that, if thrown at someone's head in the middle of the cafeteria during the seventh grade when you're just minding your own business eating beef stroganoff and sitting all by yourself, can really hurt, but not nearly as much as the names one is called while the ball is flying at one's head.

Golf is definitely the most elite of all sports, because no one gets dirty and it is played on beautiful green acres of land called courses. Golf consists of 18 holes, and the object of the game is to get the small ball into each hole in as few tries as possible. The player uses an assortment of clubs (a prop that is very similar to baseball's bat, but is instead swung from the ground in an upward direction). Different clubs are used for different things and, in the case of Tiger Woods, they are used for both the game and by his wife to beat the shit out of him for sleeping around with like four billion other women.

My uncle Bert was a golf pro at the local country club in my hometown and for a very weird summer of my life I decided to get into golf, mainly because I discovered that you got to wear a single glove like Michael Jackson and hang around middle-aged women who were drunk in the middle of the day.

In the game, you are expected to play the full 18 holes, or nine if you're playing half, or two if you're playing with the 12-

year-old gay kid that I once was. As with the other sports, someone is declared a winner.

Basketball

Much to my surprise, this game has nothing to do with hand-
woven baskets and literally nothing to do with Easter or the
bunny who represents it. The name comes from the fact that the
ball is dribbled across the court with the goal of throwing it way
up to a net formation called a basket.

Players tend to be extremely tall and always very, very
sweaty. The professional game is played indoors and, not to
bring it back to Whoopi Goldberg again, but my closest connection to the sport came when she made a movie about it
called *Eddie*. It's an *OK* movie, not bad for a '90s Whoopi
movie. Honestly, it came out during that rough period of like
three Whoopi movies a year when you were lucky when even
one of them wasn't completely bat shit insane.

For the more daring and experienced of Heterosexual
Watchers, I suggest going undercover in a disguise to one of
these boys' nights or girls' nights, depending on the gender
you're most interested in observing. For the girls' night, borrow
a basic jumper or wrap skirt from any female friend or from
your male friend who performs as Miss Anita Drink on Satur-
days at a place called Hamburger Mary's in West Hollywood.
For the boys' night, throw on any sports-related jersey and
baseball cap, but *please remember* to know what team the hat

is for. I can't tell you the number of times I've been caught in public wearing a New York Yankees hat, only to be asked by a random Heterosexual, "Did you see the game last night?" In this event, the Heterosexual will assume you know what he's talking about and, frankly, it really is your fault for wearing the hat to begin with. Unless you're fully prepared to answer team-related questions, I recommend buying a hat with no team logo printed on it. The Gap has some *really* cute pastel-colored hats on sale right now.

Feeling overwhelmed by all this Heterosexual talk? Don't be. I'm here to help. When I first started Heterosexual Watching, I was just as confused as you. I'd look at these loving creatures and wonder, "Huh?!" By this point in the book, you can probably guess that I obviously didn't have many friends growing up; as a result, I watched *a lot* of television. Specifically sitcoms. The art of the sitcom has done wonders for Heterosexual Watchers like myself, giving us a direct, intimate glimpse into the Heterosexual Married Couple (page 38), the Single Wannabe Carrie Bradshaw Female (page 31), and on the popular show *Sabrina, the Teenage Witch*, the Heterosexual Teenage Witch living with two supernatural spinsters and a talking cat.

Here is a direct transcript from my interview with a very nice Heterosexual Female I met at the gym, during which I get to the bottom of whether what I've learned about Heterosexuals from television is true or false.

Me: So, I've seen pretty much every episode of *Friends*.

HF: Me, too!

Me: Do you feel that *Friends* accurately depicts the Heterosexual lifestyle?

HF: I guess.

Me: Are you more of a Monica or a Phoebe?

HF: Hmm.

Me: Don't tell me you're a Rachel! I did *not* peg you for a Rachel.

HF: I really don't know.

Me: And that's not because you're black. It's a personality thing. In the first episode, Rachel gets cold feet on her wedding day and runs away from the church in her wedding dress and takes refuge in a locally owned coffee shop with very comfortable-looking furniture. Have you ever done that?

HF: Nope.

Me: Running away from weddings still in the dress seems to be a very common theme among many depictions of the Heterosexual Lifestyle. Julia Roberts rides away on a horse in *Runaway Bride*. Would you say that most Heterosexuals are good at horseback riding?

HF: I don't know. I can ride a horse, but I grew up around a lot of animals.

Me: OK. So all Heterosexuals can ride horses.

HF: I didn't say that.

Me: On *Friends*, Monica accidentally gets a turkey stuck on her head while preparing for Thanksgiving. Have you ever had a turkey on your head? And do you find that this is a popular activity among Heterosexuals?

HF: No, I haven't, and I don't know if that's something a lot of people do. It seems as if it'd be dangerously unsanitary so I can't imagine that anyone has actually ever done that.

Me: *Ha*. OK.

HF: What?

Me: That's just *such* a Monica thing to say.

So, in conclusion, yes. *Friends* is a 100 percent accurate depiction of the Heterosexual Lifestyle. Speaking of Jennifer Aniston,* did you know that noted Heterosexual John Mayer has dated not only Jennifer, but also Taylor Swift, Katy Perry, Jennifer Love Hewitt, Jessica Simpson, and my own mother? OK. Not the last one but, hey, there's still time. Right, Mom?

John Mayer has a lot going for him. For one, he's insanely talented and famous, and two, back in 2009 he was sizzling hot; having been hot in 2009 can really go a long way for Heterosexual Males. Just ask Gerard Butler. It's unfair to compare the common Heterosexual Male's mating rituals to that of John Mayer; he's a special case that should be studied, in depth, by the Centers for Disease Control and Prevention.

---

*That is how I begin most conversations.

How the Heterosexual Male
Attracts a Mate

The following, however, *is* how the common Heterosexual Male approaches mating, adopting one of the intriguingly different approaches outlined below.

Dating

A practice whereby one Heterosexual asks another of the opposite sex to spend time together, usually alone in a mating- or proto-mating pair. In modern times, initiation of this behavior is no longer a gender-specific phenomenon. The Heterosexual Female can ask out the male, or vice versa. When the male does the asking, these "dates" usually include dinner at a restaurant that "only locals go to," which he claims to have heard about from a friend but found in the *Zagat Restaurant Guide* he received as a Secret Santa gift at work last Christmas. For other dates, the male often takes the female to see a movie he knows she wants to see, and secretly wants to see himself. *Everybody* can appreciate Ryan Gosling!

Scent

Like many other members of the animal kingdom, the Heterosexual Male understands that scent is a medium of attraction. However, most Heterosexual Males don't want to spend an arm and a leg on high-priced cologne. Instead, Heterosexual Males resort to a substance called Axe Body Spray, a low-cost perfume marketed specifically to Heterosexual Males through commercials where the body spray transforms women into psychotic nymphomaniacs who seem to somehow have keys to every man in America's home and use said keys to break in while he's taking a shower. I don't know about you, but if six sexed-up ladies burst into my bathroom while I was taking a shower just because of the kind of body wash I had chosen to use, I would (A) call the police and scream like a little girl until they got there, and (B) quickly rethink my body wash products. While the actual result of using Axe Body Spray is never as intense as advertised, the body spray *is* rather attractive to the Heterosexual Female, presumably, at least given her alternatives.

His "Good Shirt"

Most Heterosexual Males own something each calls his "good shirt." The "good shirt" is an attractive and stylish shirt purchased on sale at Express two years earlier (to wear to his cousin Lisa's wedding or funeral; Lisa had a weird 2011). The Heterosexual Female is impressed by the gesture such self-adornment represents and, as their mating rituals accelerate, she will see more of this shirt, until she finally breaks down and buys him a second "good shirt," followed quickly by a third.

His Best High School Sports Story

Even if they didn't play a high school sport, all Heterosexual Males claim to have been "the best player on the team." The Heterosexual Male uses his sporting glory days to lure a prospective female into believing he is some kind of athletic superhuman. The Heterosexual Female can expect to hear phrases like, "People still talk about my throw" or "And everyone started cheering, 'Charlie! Charlie!' But I just kept running for the ball" or "They were really serious about my going professional, but I was just too interested in working at my dad's hardware store."

How the Heterosexual Female Attracts a Mate

On the opposite end of the spectrum, Heterosexual Females prefer much more strategic approaches to mating. However, if a Heterosexual Female seriously likes the male, she will actively try to seal the romantic deal, oftentimes resorting to ultimatums; as a reference point, listen to Beyoncé's hit song "Single Ladies," in which she tells the male in question that if he liked "it" then he should have put a ring on "it." The "it" in question here is obviously her ring finger, but it's a bigger message than this, the message being that Heterosexual Females rightfully know what they want and go for it. Also that Beyoncé is Fierce with a capital F.

The Initial Encounter

This early interaction sets the tone for the entire mating process. When the female portrays herself as shy, subdued, or hard to get, the male must woo her with mixed CDs,* greeting cards that play Taylor Swift songs, and phrases like *deep connection*. This process can prove to be immensely expensive and tiring for the male. In the case of a more aggressive Heterosexual Female or one with the helpful assistance of alcohol, the female may come on quite strong, igniting a more fast-paced mating process

---

*Mixed CDs are very popular among Heterosexuals in the courting phase and will always include the Céline Dion song "My Heart Will Go On."

that is usually welcomed by the Heterosexual Male. This female is sometimes deemed by society as "easy," which is considered both highly derogatory and a reason for giving someone a reality television show.

Primping

The Heterosexual Female beautifully decorates herself with makeup, trendy clothing, jewelry, styled hair, and perfume. A good indication of the female's interest in the male is just how much time she's spent on her appearance. If a Heterosexual Female shows up on a date in sweatpants and a Mets cap, it's safe to assume her interest is relatively low or that she is a lesbian of the butch persuasion. However, if she shows up dressed like Sandy in the last scene of *Grease** after she gets all cool and sexy and wears a leather jacket and Rizzo may or may not have lost the baby she was freaking out about in the scene before, it's safe to assume the female is either very interested or secretly a drag queen.

....

*Grease is an important movie to note, as it's one of those movies both Heterosexuals and Non-Heterosexuals alike can agree on. Oftentimes, when a Non-Heterosexual is hanging out with Heterosexuals, he will accidentally bring up a musical he's recently seen. The Heterosexual will stare at him blankly and the only way to keep the conversation moving is to say "It's a lot like *Grease*," at which point the Heterosexual will happily nod in understanding and you can continue talking about having recently seen *Les Misérables*. It's also worth noting, for no other reason than my own ego, that I was in three different productions of *Grease* all before my 18th birthday.

Facebook-Stalking

While this activity is practiced by both genders, the female nearly always outperforms the male. In order to weed out the duds, many females will research a possible mate on Facebook, discovering everything about his past and present, his favorite movies, and how fat he was in college. Warning: Heterosexuals should wait a minimum of two weeks before poking their possible mate and an additional three weeks before following him on Instagram. (Too many filtered photos of brunch dishes and your neighbor's puppy have never helped anybody find the love of her life, ladies!)

Common Interests

This can come from Facebook-stalking or from a good old-fashioned conversation; either way, when the female discovers an interest of her male counterpart, she will often use this to her advantage, claiming to also have enjoyed the first three seasons of *The Wire* and that, she, too, thinks Jet Skis are "totally awesome."

This practice can prove both successful and highly dangerous. My friend Colleen once really, really liked a guy and discovered from some serious Facebook-stalking that he was extremely into dirt bikes. I immediately warned Colleen that men with dirt bikes are just one step above men who wear raccoon tails from their belts as a fashion accessory. She didn't listen and instead claimed to be obsessed with dirt bikes, too. Colleen was in an arm brace and leg cast within a week. By lying and not

Other Uses of Facebook for the Heterosexual Female

 Tagging herself at Mexican restaurants with the caption "Hanging with my girls!"

 "Like-ing" anything her funny gay friends say or post, and then commenting, "OMG. *You are so funny!*," be it a funny viral video or simply "It's a nice day out."

 Keeping up with girls from college, but secretly hoping they're all fat and single.

 Keeping up with girls from high school, but secretly hoping they're all fat and single.

 Sharing photos of male models or celebrities with the caption "Mama like!"

 Generally referring to herself as *Mama*, despite the fact that she's 22 and doesn't have children.

Complaining about footwear.

 Posting messages about how great her boyfriend or husband is while sitting on a couch next to said boyfriend or husband.

 Getting unhealthily involved in the comments section of the L'Oreal Facebook page.

 Spending upwards of three hours exploring her ex-boyfriend's new girlfriend's pictures from Disney World. Then crying.

 Passively venting about a friend who is clearly on Facebook and meant to see said venting. For example: "Sarah is *over* the haters. You think someone is your friend after working at Nordstrom's together for two-plus years and then you hear the things she's been saying about you and realize the monster she really is."

 Posting photos of her "celebrity doppelgänger."

 Pretending her "celebrity doppelgänger" is Katie Holmes and not Kathy Bates.

being her true self, Colleen not only screwed things up with a guy she really liked, but also injured herself so badly she had to miss *The Sound of Music Sing-Along* at the Hollywood Bowl, which we had tickets to go to the following weekend. So guess who had to go out in public as Kurt von Trapp in lederhosen without his Brigitta anywhere in sight? Whatever. It's fine, Colleen. I'm over it now.

Other Heterosexuals randomly meet their mates at social functions due to happenstance or fate. Such social functions include bars, hip-hop listening parties, the park, or cocktail parties. At some point in all of our lives, we will find ourselves at a Heterosexual cocktail party.* *Do not panic and do not be alarmed.* That is the all-time worst way to begin the evening. Or any evening for that matter. Panicking at cocktail parties is like sitting through an entire episode of *The Good Wife*: After a few glasses of wine, sure, it seems like a good idea, but ultimately it just isn't worth it.

---

*I have blacked out at almost every Heterosexual cocktail party I've ever attended.

What to Expect at a Heterosexual Cocktail Party

A Heterosexual cocktail party can be lots of fun if you know what to expect; some of my favorite nights have been at Heterosexual cocktail parties. Obviously, they serve as a great place for some in-depth Heterosexual Watching.

Presliced Cheese Platters

Heterosexuals love those trays of cheese that have already been sliced when you buy them from the prepared-food deli case at the store. Even if they've gone to the effort to move the presliced cheese onto actual dishware, do not be fooled; this cheese was cut long before they bought it, and, no, that wasn't a fart joke. Farting at cocktail parties, by the way, is usually frowned upon.

What Should I Bring?

Good question. A bottle of wine is a perfectly respectable gift,* and if you want to think outside the box, consider a scented candle or a decorative figurine. Heterosexuals love those candles that smell like baked goods and any sort of Precious Moments figurine. Gifts to avoid include edible clothing of any

----

*Gifts your Heterosexual hosts won't appreciate: tickets to the national tour of *The Drowsy Chaperone*; photos of yourself dressed as a shirtless cowboy, no matter how much you've been working out; livestock; an autographed copy of Teri Garr's memoir, *Speedbumps: Flooring It Through Hollywood*.

Heterosexual Gift-Giving

While we're on the topic of gifts, at some point you will likely be searching for a gift to give the Heterosexuals in your life, either for Christmas, a birthday, or as an apology for spilling that pitcher of white Russians all over their brand new couch. Fear not! Consider one of the following suggestions:

Homemade bread: Heterosexuals will be touched by the notion that you took the time to make them bread; plus, if you are a Non-Heterosexual, Heterosexuals are always impressed by Non-Heterosexuals with good cooking skills. Even if you can't bake bread, go to your local bakery, buy something fresh, take it home, wrap it in foil, and call it your own. The Heterosexual will say things like, "Jeffery is such a good baker! Gay people are great!" for weeks to come.

Gift cards: Heterosexuals love gift cards because you're putting the decision in their hands. Stores all Heterosexuals love include Best Buy, Pier 1, Barnes & Noble, anywhere that sells dog clothing, and Target. Stores to avoid include locally owned Russian bookstores, Big & Tall stores, and places that only sell bootleg DVDs.

This book: Heterosexuals will love receiving a copy of this book for two reasons: (1) because Heterosexuals *love* reading about themselves, and (2) they'll appreciate that you're sharing something you love so intensely, and something that President Barack Obama has declared "vital reading for the general public."*

*Barack Obama may or may not know I exist.

Gadgets: Heterosexuals appreciate gadgets more than anyone else. So why not give them the latest electric back scratcher or battery-operated coaster that keeps coffee warm? Purchase a plane ticket to anywhere, board the plane, take your complimentary copy of *Sky Mall* magazine, and as soon as you arrive at your destination, start shopping!

Cash: Obviously.

Whiskey: If the Heterosexual you're shopping for is anything like my dad, just buy him a nice bottle of whiskey, and it'll be the best gift he's received all year. I don't think my sister and I have gotten my dad a non-alcoholic Christmas gift since we were 13.

Socks: All Heterosexuals need socks, unless they don't have feet; in that case, I would suggest avoiding socks at all costs.

Edible Arrangements: Heterosexuals love to receive Edible Arrangements, flowerlike arrangements made out of fruit. I've never quite gotten the allure of this phenomenon, but Heterosexuals seem to go crazy for them. That said, wake me up when somebody comes up with a Drinkable Arrangement.

kind, Rita Wilson's *AM/FM* CD, or, worst of all, do not regift the bottle of peach liqueur the hosts gave you for your birthday. I don't care how much space it is taking up in your freezer; they will remember, and they will be hurt.

Music

It isn't going to be your taste, but ignore that and enjoy it. A little John Mayer never hurt anybody. Well, actually, I think he hurt Taylor Swift and I can only assume Jennifer Aniston, but who *hasn't* hurt Jennifer Aniston? I promise that is the last time I'm going to bring up John Mayer and Jennifer Aniston.*

Conversation

Get ready to talk about stuff you absolutely couldn't care less about. I'm talking the Mets; I'm talking the economy; I'm talking why the Droid** is better than the iPhone. But you might learn some things, so listen. Making idle conversation with drunk Heterosexuals at a cocktail party is a great way to gain insight into their culture, and it's also a good way to catch up on what's been happening on ABC's *Bachelor Pad*.

---

*Just kidding. I can't promise that!

**Heterosexual Males love the Droid, as it's a phone specifically marketed to them. Watch a Droid commercial, and you'll quickly realize that they are about as Heterosexual as the Super Bowl. Even the sound they make: DROOOOID. It's so overtly masculine and aggressive. Every time I hear a man turn on a Droid, I think, *we get it*—you have a penis and you like putting it inside women. Now, can I go back to reading this Tim Gunn biography?

The Top 10 Things You Should Avoid While at a Heterosexual Cocktail Party

1. Cher impressions. I don't care how great your friends tell you yours is, Heterosexuals will not care and also, to be honest, it isn't *that* great.

2. Asking the Heterosexual Female host, "Are those real?"

3. Pretty much anything having to do with the Tony Awards.

4. Asking who has drugs, then saying you're kidding, then saying, "No, but really."

5. Saying, "Fuck the Beatles."

6. Putting on a wig midway into the party—or at any point during the party, for that matter.

7. Showing up already wearing a wig. You might think it's cute. The other guests will not.

8. Asking the hosts if they have any wigs.

9. Inviting 15 of your closest friends whose names you don't remember.

10. Pretending you're choking so the host's boyfriend will give you mouth to mouth, then, right as he does, sticking your tongue down his throat and saying, "*Gotcha!*"

How Late Should I Plan to Stay?

Customarily, Heterosexual cocktail parties end on the earlier side, so don't overstay your welcome. The hosts might casually suggest that they'd "better take Mindy out." Mindy is the Heterosexuals' dog, who will one day be completely forgotten and ignored once said Heterosexual hosts have a baby. Once the "walk the dog" line has been used, or the obligatory yawn stifled, you should politely leave. This is the end of the night, and just because you think cocktail parties should end with your showing everyone YouTube clips of girls in beauty pageants falling down does *not* mean others feel the same way.

Don't Forget to Say Thank-You!

You should now thank your hosts and leave the cocktail party, and, by all means, do *not*, under any circumstances, take the bottle of wine you brought with you, just because it never got opened and just because liquor stores have all closed for the night and you literally don't even have a beer at home and you've told everyone still there that you're having an after-party at your place; this does not mean it is socially acceptable to take the bottle home with you. Just say thank-you, go home, and for God's sake, go to bed; you have to work in the morning!

What to Expect at a Straight Bar

A Heterosexual cocktail party is much different from its sister encounter, Attending a Heterosexual Bar or Nightclub. Heterosexual behavior and protocol can be quite different in a person's home than it is in a public setting. You will encounter far more intoxicated strangers at a Heterosexual Bar or Nightclub, and also, at a Heterosexual Bar, it's extremely hard to control the television remote control. While at a Heterosexual's home, you can casually pick up the remote and change it from ESPN* to the night's top stories on Rachel Maddow, or, in my case, a rerun of *Veronica's Closet* on the TV Guide Channel. However, at a bar, you will be forced to sweet-talk a heavyset woman named Ginger who's busy making whiskey sours, unless you're cool with watching the Packers versus Bears game for the next five hours. To prepare you for what you should expect at a straight bar, I am going to share my journal account of a recent trip.

---

*ESPN is a TV channel solely dedicated to broadcasting sports 24/7. It's like what CNN does for news, and what Bravo does for drunk women and gay guys.

9:15 pm: My boyfriend and I predrink at our place, both to save money and also to continue watching the vintage Reba McEntire YouTube clips we've spent the better half of the afternoon watching.

10:15 pm: We go to the Pig and Whistle,* a bar located in Hollywood. Forging our way through a posse of loud, drunk girls, we make our way to the bar, and my boyfriend, Patrick, receives unwelcome gropes from a girl who's wearing a plastic tiara announcing that she has just turned 30. Patrick orders a Bud Light, and I request a glass of pinot noir. I am given a look from the bartender, a look I have seen in countless straight bars before. It is the look that says, "You're standing under a neon Corona sign and there are peanut shells under your feet, and yet you're seriously ordering a glass of red wine?"

*It is worth noting that only Heterosexuals would name anything *Pig and Whistle*.

114

11:00 pm: The same drunk girl wearing the tiara comes over to our table, claiming to be the "real-life Karen Walker"* and asks Patrick to dance with her. I give her a look that says, "Back off bitch," but she doesn't understand and won't go away; eventually, Patrick has no choice but to dance with her. I notice a male at the bar smile and wink at a female on the opposite end of the bar. I realize this is considered Heterosexual Courting.

(Continued on page 116)

11:30 pm: Someone is handing out tequila shots for April's birthday (the girl in the tiara), and because Patrick danced with her, we are handed two of them. Each. We drink them. Both.

*Anytime anyone claims to be the "real-life" anybody from a television show, do not believe him/her; if claiming it was all it took, I would have magically morphed into Aunt Jackie from *Roseanne* years ago.

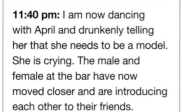

11:40 pm: I am now dancing with April and drunkenly telling her that she needs to be a model. She is crying. The male and female at the bar have now moved closer and are introducing each other to their friends.

(Continued from page 115)

12:32 am: I'm dizzy, and we've spent the past 15 minutes trying to leave but, for some reason, ever since we told April we're gay, she has been ignoring all her actual friends and incessantly telling us about her gay friend from high school who now manages an American Apparel in Tempe, Arizona. "You guys would love each other!" she keeps shouting.

12:55 am: I am shocked to see the Heterosexual Male casually touch the female's backside and am even more shocked when she turns around, smacks him in the face and leaves; in my culture when such a move is made, it is universally understood that you will now be boyfriends for the next two days. After the female goes, I notice another female approach the same male, smile at him, and they leave together. I am thoroughly impressed.

1:30 am: Having now been treated like gay kings by drunken April, and April having actively pissed off just about all the friends she came in with, we decide it is time to head home. Inevitably, when I wake up the next morning, I will discover that I drunkenly friended April on Facebook and was tagged in 12 pictures, in eight of which I'm wearing the plastic tiara. April will message me for the next week about hanging out again before she realizes that I'm probably never going to write her back and gives up. Also, I'm hungover for the next 48 hours. Straight People know how to drink.

Now, let's jump ahead. Imagine if you will that those two Heterosexuals that I saw flirting at the bar had liked each other. Let's pretend that when the male touched the female's backside, she wasn't offended. What would have happened next? Marriage, you say? Not that easily, unless, of course, they're 20-something celebrities or drunk in Las Vegas. However, once the courting process is complete, Heterosexuals can then eagerly close the deal and solidify their relationship with marriage.

If you've seen *Father of the Bride*,* part 1, you know that marriage is a beautiful thing. You also know that early-1990s Diane Keaton is basically everything you need to know about style and motherhood. However, if the Heterosexuals in your life decide to tie the knot, you'll soon be attending a Heterosexual Wedding, and if you're not ready, you will find yourself *extremely* confused by everything from who catches the bouquet to what isn't OK to say to the bride.

---

*If you haven't seen *Father of the Bride*, part 1, we have nothing to discuss; same thing goes for part 2, by the way.

What to Expect at a Heterosexual Wedding

Heterosexuals have the unique right to get married, and they take this right very seriously. There is an entire industry surrounding Heterosexual weddings, from wedding planners, bridal stores, Céline Dion love songs, bridal registries,* and a plethora of divorce attorneys. The world is ripe for Heterosexual nuptials.

Here are some key things you should know going in:

- You must remember that a Heterosexual wedding is the most important day of the Heterosexual's life, and it is *no* time for sarcasm or self-aware comedy. No matter how hilariously sarcastic you may be, the bride will *not* find it funny if you raise your hand in the middle of the ceremony for the "Does anyone object?" part. Even if you're wearing fingerless gloves and a shirt that the bride bought you for your 25th birthday, and even if you were personally invited because you're the bride's "funniest friend." It is not OK. Consider this my apology, Katherine.

---

*Registering for gifts is one of the weirdest things that Heterosexuals do. This is the process by which Heterosexuals will go to a store and make a list of things their friends and family are expected to buy for them. It's a really weird way to give a gift; however, if you're ever feeling down, I highly suggest going to the dishware section of Bloomingdale's and creating an entire wedding registry for yourself and Joseph Gordon-Levitt.

- Music at a Heterosexual wedding can go either way. Some Heterosexuals stick to traditional "wedding music" played on a piano or organ, while others step outside the box. I once attended a Heterosexual wedding where the bride made her way down the aisle to the expected "Here Comes the Bride," only to stop midway, pull out a wireless microphone, and sing "Can't Help Falling in Love with You" in the middle of the church, and then proceeded to the altar as if nothing had happened. It was live theater at its most dramatic. No matter what the music choices may be, it is best to pretend that every single song played is your favorite song of all time, or else the bride will become agitated and call you a few weeks later to tell you that you ruined her day. Again, Katherine, I am *sorry*. You were right. Neil Young *is* the voice of love.

- Depending on the time of day the wedding is taking place, you will be expected to dress up. I recommend wearing a suit no matter what, because it's always better to be the best-dressed guy there than "that guy who showed up in the Madonna Confessions Tour T-shirt and white jeans." In my defense, the invitation said *casual,* and you know that, Katherine.

- A reception will follow, where people get extremely drunk and make total asses of themselves; however, that doesn't mean you have to, as well. A local deejay named something like Skeeter or Mickey Jive or Pooter will be on hand, or, in the case of a more expensive wedding, a live band with a wedding singer covering some of the most beloved and romantic Heterosexual songs of all time, songs like "Faithfully" by Journey, "Could I Have This Dance" by Anne Murray, or "Funky Town" by Lipps Inc.

- At the reception, food will be served, as well as a wedding cake with miniature figurines of the bride and groom on top. No matter how funny you think it might be to position the bride figurine's face on the groom figurine's crotch, that is a *really* bad idea. Even though people might be egging you on and even though you may have had so many tequila sunrises that you left all sense of dignity in Funky Town, it is a *really* bad idea. A bad idea that can serve as the final straw with someone you spent four years living with when you first moved to the city and whom you used to call your best friend.

- The reception will end with the bride throwing her bouquet to a swarm of single women. The Heterosexual tradition is that whoever catches the bride's bouquet will be the next to get married, and the women around you will take this *extremely* seriously. It is best to simply stand back and let the ladies fight it out in what, to the untrained eye, will resemble a Civil War reenactment.

- Eventually the bride and groom will leave, and everyone will throw either rice or birdseed on them. The tradition of throwing rice has become less PC, as it has been discovered that when birds eat it, their stomachs explode, and people stopped being cool with that sometime in the late '70s. The bride and groom will drive away in a car that has *Just Married* written in soap on the back window. They will go off on a honeymoon to start their lives as husband and wife, and despite the fact that the bar might still be well-stocked, you are expected to politely make your exit and not demand another tequila sunrise, and under no circumstances should you call the bartender a "self-hating shit-tard" when he announces that the bar is closed and refuses to serve you.

All in all, if you follow these rules, Heterosexual weddings can be a lot of fun. It's a beautiful thing to experience with the Heterosexuals in your life, and will serve as a great place for Heterosexual Watching, and sometimes for accidentally pissing off your best friend. Katherine, just call me. We should be able to talk about this. Please.

So, no matter what you did at their wedding, your Heterosexual friends have gotten married, and they're now husband and wife. Your relationship dynamic might change dramatically, as a Single Heterosexual Female and a Married Heterosexual Female can be very different kinds of animals. The girl you used to call at midnight on a Wednesday and say,

"Let's get margaritas!" might not respond as enthusiastically as she once did; instead, she might offer up the excuse that she has to work in the morning and that she and her husband just started watching the latest episode of *White Collar*. In more extreme cases, what tends to follow marriage is the ultimate shift in the Heterosexual lifestyle: childbirth.

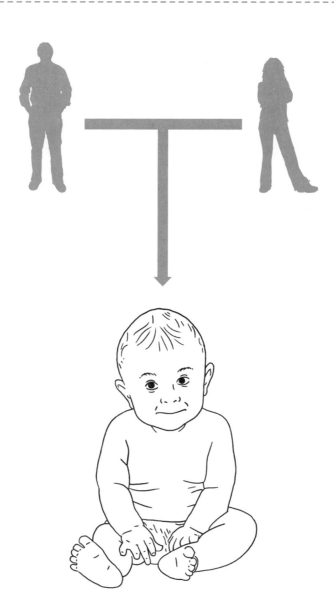

How Heterosexuals Reproduce

One of the unique qualities of Heterosexuals is their ability to reproduce by simply forgetting to wear a condom, forgetting to take a birth control pill, or simply going out to dinner with Jon Gosselin. Or, of course, in many cases, by mutually deciding that it's time to start a family with their opposite-sex partner.

The Heterosexual reproduction process is a truly amazing thing that takes nine months to happen. Here's how it works.

First, you need *two* Heterosexuals, or one Heterosexual Female and a very, very, very drunk gay guy. Sometimes, these two Heterosexuals love each other (as in the case of your newly married friends), and other times they have just met while watching the Lakers game at the Pig and Whistle bar I discovered earlier. Whether they're in love or not, if the Heterosexuals have unprotected Heterosexual intercourse,* they will likely create a baby. Heterosexual intercourse can take upwards of an hour or sometimes only a few minutes if the Heterosexual Male hasn't had a lot of action lately.

Once the seed has been planted in the egg (see, I'd look like an idiot trying to explain that), the two things combine to form a new cell called a blastocyst, which, despite how it

---

*While I am fascinated by this mating ritual, I will not attempt to explain the actual mechanics of Heterosexual sex, as I have never experienced it firsthand, and the only vagina I've ever seen is Sharon Stone's in *Basic Instinct*. And honestly, I kind of prefer her in *Casino*.

sounds, is *not* a racial slur. This blastocyst begins traveling through the fallopian tubes (this shit is crazy, right?!) toward the uterus, which takes roughly three days, which is kind of ridiculous when you realize that you can drive from Georgia to California in a matter of three days. Sure, you'd be doing a lot of driving and it's best to take shifts with a friend so you don't fall asleep at the wheel, and if you make it more like a week you get to stop in historical places like the Alamo or the World's Biggest Ball of Yarn. I know a guy who watched all the seasons of *Damages* in just three days. And by *guy*, I mean me. However, three days is the amount of time it takes to get that blasted blastocyst through those fallopian tubes and into the spacious uterus.

Once Mr. (or Ms.) Blastocyst gets to the uterus, it attaches itself onto the walls of the uterus, the way you might attach a poster of Selena Gomez to your wall if you're a teenage boy or a weird lesbian. The uterus is basically a hotel, like a really nice, comfortable hotel. Not five stars by any means, but maybe three? OK, two stars, depending on the uterus. And it's not all that spacious, either, unless you're looking at it by New York City hotel room standards, in which case it's *huge*. The view is shit, literally, but it's comfortable and the blastocyst doesn't mind staying there for roughly nine months. Once attached to the walls of this Sheraton Inn & Suites (a.k.a. the uterus), the blastocyst starts to develop into an embryo, and after four weeks it's roughly the size of a poppy seed. A poppy seed is very specific, not a sunflower seed, not a flaxseed, but a poppy seed.

Think about *that* the next time you order a poppy-seed bagel with cream cheese and lox.

Now, the female has this poppy seed attached to the uterine wall and she's figured out she's pregnant, or she hasn't, in which case her family submits her for that *I Didn't Know I Was Pregnant* reality show and she gets to proudly tell all her friends, "I'm gonna be on TV!" There's also a placenta and an umbilical cord forming, which is how the poppy seed that's gonna one day be her pissed-off teenage daughter who keeps running up her Verizon bill is able to grow.

The pregnant Heterosexual Female will start to gain weight and have extreme mood swings. One minute she might be super-happy to be alive, but the next minute she's craving pickles covered in brown gravy and blaming her spouse for everything, from making her feel so terrible to the existence of the Kardashians* in general. The female's nerves are incredibly high-strung and what she really wants is a nice stiff drink to ease her tension, but she can't do that because she's pregnant. Dammit.

Over the next several months, the pregnant Heterosexual Female goes through many other side effects. Things to expect include nausea, tiredness, tender breasts, and a sudden emotional reaction to that Taylor Swift song about moms.

---

*It would be a disservice to write a guide to Heterosexuals without at least mentioning the Kardashians. The Kardashians are a fascinating Heterosexual enigma that won't seem to go away. Like bedbugs or cancer. No matter how you feel about this celebrity family, they're doing something right. Everyone knows their names, and, for the most part, everyone has seen them naked.

As the due date approaches, the Heterosexuals get very caught up in baby fever.* Oftentimes, a family member or friend will host a baby shower, traditionally a females-only luncheon without the added bonus of booze, where everyone brings gifts and pretends to have an emotional attachment to tiny pairs of Crocs and pyramids built entirely out of diapers.

If the pregnant Heterosexual Female's mother or mother-in-law is on hand, the female will go through a series of stressful trips to Heterosexual meccas, such as Babies "R" Us. By the end of these nine months, the Heterosexual Female will have started to resent her mother and/or mother-in-law with the kind of ferocity reserved for war criminals and Red Sox fans.

The female will also begin to tire of the Heterosexual Male in her life. Everything he does will drive her crazy, and she honestly can't believe he plays the TV that loud, and what's that stupid noise he makes when he chews wasabi peas?

There's a tiny person lodged inside her, so she's increasingly uncomfortable and bloated all the time. It is during this period that the Heterosexual Female begins to wonder if she just should have gotten a parakeet instead.

Finally, the big day comes and the Heterosexual Female has her baby and all hardship is forgiven. It's highly likely she will never see her Heterosexual friends ever again, or when she does

---

*Not to be confused with *Baby Boom*, which is another great movie starring Diane Keaton. It came out a few years before the aforementioned *Father of the Bride*, part 1, but she's still flawless.

see them, she will only discuss children's bowel movements and the hit television show *Yo Gabba Gabba*. Either way, the new parents have a sweet, gorgeous newborn baby to shower with love and affection, and the great circle of life continues. And, finally, the Heterosexual Female can order herself a very well-deserved drink.

On Babies

Heterosexuals will always assume you want to hold their babies, and if you want to get through the encounter without any trouble, I highly recommend just holding the baby and saying it's the cutest thing you've ever seen, no matter how much the baby looks like an unripened apricot. Some babies aren't as cute as others, and in these instances you will need to lie, because in the eyes of Heterosexuals, there is nothing that has ever or will ever be as cute as their baby.

Understanding Heterosexuals

Understanding how the Heterosexual Male and Female brain works can give you a better understanding of how they process thoughts, feelings, interests, and emotions. This is a chart of what makes up the Heterosexual Male's brain.

The Heterosexual Male Brain

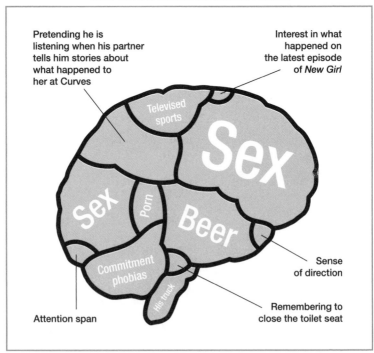

Pretending he is listening when his partner tells him stories about what happened to her at Curves

Interest in what happened on the latest episode of *New Girl*

Televised sports

Sex

Sex

Porn

Beer

Commitment phobias

His truck

Sense of direction

Remembering to close the toilet seat

Attention span

Very interesting, huh? Now take a look at the Heterosexual Female's brain.

The Heterosexual Female Brain

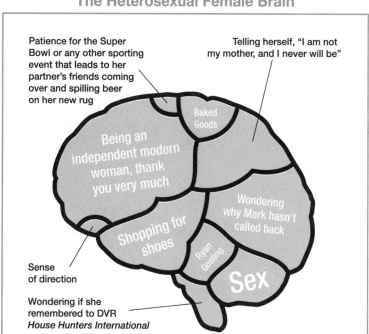

You are now prepared to deal with the major milestones in the Heterosexual Lifestyle. If you have been paying close attention, you and your Heterosexual counterparts should be able to happily coexist and continue to teach each another about your equally swell cultures.

The Heterosexual SAT #1:
Analogies

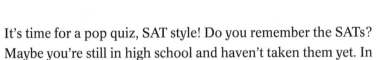

It's time for a pop quiz, SAT style! Do you remember the SATs? Maybe you're still in high school and haven't taken them yet. In which case, I'd prefer a parent or guardian or supervising adult be here with us to make me feel a little less uncomfortable.

I took the SAT on a Saturday morning after opening night of the amateur production of *Steel Magnolias* that I directed in my hometown. Suffice it to say, I pretty much flunked the SAT. Not because I'm dumb—if anything, I'm cripplingly bright—but because I was tired and, let's be honest, probably hungover. More importantly, however, I knew I didn't need the SAT to do what I wanted to do. Star on Broadway! And look at me now!*

Heterosexual SAT questions will be scattered throughout the book as a series of pop quizzes, and they're far more important and useful than the actual SAT could ever dream of being. It is vital you take these quizzes in order to continue understanding this spotter's guide, as well as honing your Heterosexual-Watching skills as we go along.

....

*The closest I've come to starring on Broadway is going on two dates with a guy who was the understudy for Danny in *Grease*, and he won't look at me anymore.

EXAMPLES:

CAT: MAMMAL as SNAKE: REPTILE
or
FISHERMAN: FISHING as
PAUL GIAMATTI: OVERACTING

Understand? If not, ask someone smarter than you to help,
then continue.

1. FRAT BOY: FRAT HOUSE ::
   A. Cowboy: Cowgirl
   B. Teacher: Book
   C. Parker Posey: Parker Posey's house
   D. Spoon: Fork

2. HIPSTER: SKINNY JEANS ::
   A. Dog: Cat
   B. New Jersey: New York
   C. Mice: Mouse
   D. Whoopi in *Sister Act*: Nun's habit

3. PARIS: FRENCH PEOPLE ::
   A. Mom: Dad
   B. *Details* magazine: *People* magazine
   C. Las Vegas: Dangerously intoxicated Heterosexuals
   D. Farm: Grass

4. METROSEXUAL: PERFECT HAIR ::
   A. Oreos: Chocolate
   B. Robert Pattinson: Extremely dirty hair
   C. Football: Super Bowl
   D. Super old: Regis Philbin

5. HETEROSEXUAL FEMALE: A BRAND-NEW SHIRTLESS
   PHOTO OF RYAN GOSLING ::
   A. Halloween: Costumes
   B. Car: Honda
   C. Water: Pool
   D. Me at age six on Christmas morning: The Play-Doh
      Magic set I'd spent all of December thinking
      about and my very own VHS copy of *Addams Family
      Values*!!!

6. HOT WINGS: HETEROSEXUAL MALES ::
   A. Ice cream: Lactose-intolerant people
   B. Hot dogs: Vegetarians
   C. White wine: *The Real Housewives of New York*
   D. M&M's: Diabetics

7. STRAIGHT PEOPLE: HETEROSEXUALS ::
   A. Dogs: Cats
   B. Students: College
   C. Winter: Summer
   D. That lady with the crazy face who used to be
      famous but does commercials for Depends Adult
      Diapers now: Lisa Rinna

8. CARRIE BRADSHAW: FABULOUS HETEROSEXUAL ICON ::
   A. Tom Cruise: Chef
   B. Roseanne Barr: Internationally beloved sex symbol
   C. President: White House
   D. Donald Trump: The world's worst Heterosexual

9. HETEROSEXUAL WEDDING: WEDDING CAKE ::
   A. Walmart: The Queen of England
   B. Rachael Ray: Speaking loudly
   C. Flowers: Bouquet
   D. The Olive Garden: Bottomless salads and breadsticks

10. HETEROSEXUAL WATCHING: HETEROSEXUAL ::
    A. Halle Berry: Watching Halle Berry's Oscar speech on YouTube at least once a day
    B. Baseball: Guy watching baseball
    C. Bird-watching: Birds
    D. Halle Berry: Watching *Monster's Ball*, the movie Halle Berry won an Oscar for at least *twice* a day

ANSWERS:

Chapter 4

Heterosexual Migration Patterns

HETEROSEXUAL MIGRATION PATTERNS ARE USUALLY HIGHLY specific to their breeds. On any given day, thousands of Heterosexuals can be found migrating to warm environments and world-famous cities, taking a break from their usual lifestyle, and trying something new, like eating pho! The following are the most popular migration destinations within the Heterosexual community.

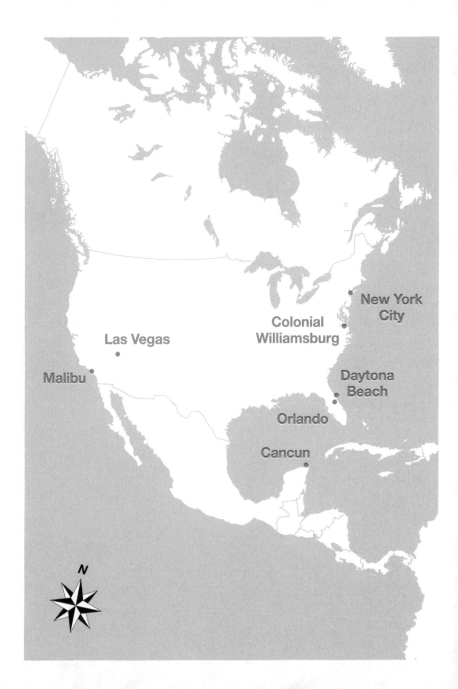

The Destinations

Las Vegas

This is one of the most popular Heterosexual migration spots, and for many reasons. It is a city designed for people who don't want to do too much walking or standing, and what better way to relax than to sit at a Crocodile Dundee slot machine and drink bottomless Bloody Marys?

Local entertainment is geared to the Heterosexual: chippendale shows for the ladies and topless bars for the men, then throw in the comedy of Rita Rudner for the older crowd, and Donny and Marie Osmond's never-ending concert act for everyone in between.

Did anyone say *hungry*? Las Vegas offers some of the world's least healthy food. Heterosexuals can find all-you-can-eat buffets at the entrance of every casino, along with restaurants owned by chefs the Heterosexual will recognize from television. Best of all, any of these food options can be delivered to your hotel room at any hour of the day. Heterosexuals in Vegas don't have to take time out of watching a Morgan Freeman* movie on Pay-Per-View to do pesky things like sitting down for dinner or walking down the street.

....

*Morgan Freeman is an older African-American male whom Heterosexuals time and time again hire to play God in their movies, leaving future civilizations to believe that the Almighty Creator of the Universe is also the guy who drove Jessica Tandy around in *Driving Miss Daisy*.

WARNING:

Anyone other than Heterosexuals should avoid Las Vegas at all costs (especially the Homosexual, despite the allure of Cher's long-running Caesars Palace concert stint). More than an hour in this place will leave you questioning all sorts of things like the future of humanity, women's right to choose, and just how much money Cher* really needs.

Orlando

Orlando is to the Heterosexual family what Las Vegas is to the Heterosexual alcoholic. Orlando is one of the strangest things about human civilization, stranger than dogs wearing shoes or Tilda Swinton's personal life. Made popular by Disney World, Orlando offers all sorts of Heterosexual destinations, such as Universal Studios, SeaWorld, and some place called Gatorland, which is exactly what it sounds like it is. The city sits in the swampy central part of Florida and exists for one purpose: to entertain the Heterosexual family.

On any given day, Orlando is visited by thousands upon thousands of Heterosexuals traveling halfway across the world to ride rides, eat food on sticks, and take pictures with a man

*While Cher is, in fact, a Heterosexual, she does not belong to the species. Cher belongs 100 percent to gay men. More so than most gay men. Myself included.

who is dressed as Captain Hook and was once an MFA student in modern dance at Juilliard. It is here that the Heterosexual can proudly flaunt his or her lifestyle by pushing a tandem baby stroller while wearing cargo shorts.*

Daytona Beach

Daytona Beach is another Florida-based popular migration spot for the Heterosexual. Here you will find the overweight Heterosexual in a swimsuit, drinking frozen drinks, and blaring their native music (by artists such as Lynyrd Skynyrd or Limp Bizkit). Groups of Heterosexuals gather in Daytona Beach to tan their normally pale skin, eat fried shrimp, and buy novelty T-shirts that say things like *Don't talk to me until I've had my coffee!* and *FBI: Female Body Inspector.* If one is looking to see Larry the Cable Guy live in concert (and what Heterosexual isn't?), his best bet would be checking out the Daytona Beach cultural arts calendar.

New York City

The Heterosexual Female *loves* visiting New York City because it makes her feel like a real-life Carrie Bradshaw, even though Carrie Bradshaw never flew in from Chattanooga, Tennessee, to stay at the Times Square Holiday Inn Express. This is obviously a popular destination among the Single Wannabe Carrie Bradshaw Female (page 31), but its appeal goes even further, making

----

*As I mentioned earlier, Heterosexuals love their pockets. So when shopping for a Heterosexual, remember: the more pockets the better.

the simplest of Heterosexuals feel decadent and fabulous. The Heterosexual Female really lets loose in New York City, staying out too late and drinking very sugary alcoholic drinks at bars with names like Area and Tunnel. These females will return to their native habitats with stories of their drunken hookup with a real-live New Yorker they met at one of the previously named bars before going to his studio apartment in Jersey City.

Cancun

The Heterosexual visits Cancun to celebrate an annual holiday called Spring Break. Spring Break comes from the collegiate term for "a weeklong holiday taking place between the months following winter and preceding summer." During this time, young Heterosexuals retreat to the warm waters of Cancun for unlimited Coronas and bad decisions. Bad decisions made in Cancun include, but are not limited to, participation in wet T-shirt contests,* *Girls Gone Wild* video appearances, and getting pregnant by someone from Wyoming. Cancun is a place for the Heterosexual to unwind by running rampant in a drunken, unsterile mating frenzy on the not-so-white beaches of Mexico.

---

*A wet T-shirt contest is an exhibitionist competition where Heterosexual Females wear white or light-colored T-shirts with nothing underneath, and allow someone to pour water on them, causing the shirts to cling to their exposed breasts, and feminists everywhere to roll over in their hypothetical graves. A team of judges, or the crowd's reaction, will determine who wins. I've never been to a wet T-shirt contest, and it ranks on my list of Things I Never Want to See, just after World War III and Kevin James without pants on.

Colonial Williamsburg

Heterosexuals looking to take in a little history and culture on their migration, by which I mean old people and nerds, will migrate to Colonial Williamsburg. This old-fashioned city is a Heterosexual history buff's fantasy land, as this place is full of old-time buildings and hired actors wearing period clothing and pretending to be from the early 1700s. Colonial Williamsburg is one of the last places in America where someone can legitimately claim to be a blacksmith* for a living.

Malibu

We all know Malibu Barbie, but did you know that Malibu Barbie was inspired by the countless Heterosexuals who migrate to Malibu's beautiful beaches on a yearly basis? It's true, Barbie *is* a Heterosexual, albeit 50 years old and made of plastic. Malibu is basically the opposite of Cancun; this is a quiet, stylish, posh beach where Heterosexuals looking to have a decadent beach experience and get photographed by the paparazzi will migrate. I live in Los Angeles, and of the few Heterosexuals I speak to on a daily basis (not intentional, I've just pissed *a lot* of people off), they all migrate to Malibu. Recently, I tagged along on one such Heterosexual Migration.

....

*A blacksmith is an old-time profession whereby one creates objects out of steel or wrought iron, which, in modern times, is often confused with Will Smith, an African-American actor who just so happens to have the last name *Smith*.

My Day at the Beach with Heterosexuals

11:31 am: I am writing from the comfort of my home, where I am holed up rewatching the first season of *Lost*. I always go back and try to watch this show from the beginning, but then end up giving up around season 3. I still have no idea what happens in the season finale. But don't tell me. I already got the *Cheers* finale ruined for me, which I've been putting off watching for years because ultimately I'm not in the emotional headspace to say good-bye to Sam Malone yet.

12:49 pm: Two Heterosexual Females I know have picked up my boyfriend and me. This will be the first Heterosexual beach experience I've had since going to Pensacola, Florida, with my parents in 1997.

1:42 pm: We arrive in Malibu. The first thing I notice about this Heterosexual beach party is the overwhelming supply of beer kept in an empty trash can full of ice. I doubt it's how Nate Berkus would serve beer, but I accept the ice-cold cans nonetheless.

1:50 pm: I finish two beers and am roped into playing a game involving more beer. They call this game Beer Pong, whereby two teams compete to make the opposing team drink as much beer as is physically possible. An entire rating system (too complex to explain here*) is set to determine how many points each team gets and how long one must drink.

(Continued on page 148)

1:56 pm: I have now consumed three beers since beginning the game.

2:00 pm: These Heterosexuals have an innate ability to chug beer like no other species. I'm having a hard time doing this, by which I mean I've now managed to lose four beanbags by accidentally tossing them into the ocean. The Heterosexuals are patient with me as I lose a fifth one.

*I just didn't understand the rating system.

145

What is Beer Pong and how do I play?

The best advice I can give any Heterosexual spotter trying to learn how to play Beer Pong is to enroll in any undergraduate program across America. Beer Pong is to college students as screaming over each other so much that they barely make any point at all is to the cohosts of *The View*.

But you didn't tell me what it is.

You're right. Sorry. I got carried away thinking about *The View*. But while we're on the topic of drinking games, here's one you might try. The next time you find yourself watching *The View* and having an alcoholic beverage (which shouldn't be too often since *The View* is a morning talk show and drinking that early in the day is a pretty good sign that you have a problem), take a big swig of your drink every time Whoopi rolls her eyes in disgust at Barbara Walters. Seriously. Try it. You will have alcohol poisoning by the time they get to the first guest.

Much like my *View* drinking game, the object of Beer Pong is to get your fellow players utterly smashed. Two teams compete to land a small plastic ball in each other's cups. Each time Team A lands a ball in their cup, Team B must chug the cup full of beer, then back and forth until someone wins or passes out.

What should I expect at a game of Beer Pong?

Pandemonium similar to the first scene after they drop off all the tributes in *The Hunger Games*, minus the blood, graphic deaths, and ominous but really well-written film score. Heterosexuals unleash something inside themselves the minute they begin a game such as Beer Pong, and, if played correctly, it can be almost as much fun as watching *The Hunger Games* and imagining what would happen if the tributes were the cohosts of *The View*.

A large supply of plastic Solo Cups, the stamina to handle excessive beer consumption, a designated driver, and a tomorrow that can be spent recovering in front of your TV with a bottle of ibuprofen, some Gatorade, and, if you're like me . . . an episode of *The View*.

The Top Five Ways a Game of Beer Pong Is Similar to *The View*

1. Both led me to skip a countless number of classes while in college.

2. It's best to start both having had at least one or two drinks before. To loosen up.

3. Something tells me Rosie O'Donnell is skilled at both.

4. Both lead people to scream belligerently at each other.

5. Both could potentially kill Barbara Walters.

2:31 pm: Someone has won the game, and many of the Hetero-sexual Males are angry. They claim that the other team cheated, and cite me as a team handicap. I begin to protest, but accidentally knock over the two slates of wood that make up our game and opt against it.

3:00 pm: The Heterosexuals and I migrate to the beach. I get another beer and declare out loud, to no one in particular, "I'm having a very good time."

(Continued from page 145)

3:06 pm: Someone points out that the swimsuit I'm wearing basically matches the bikini of the Heterosexual Female sitting next to me. I'm both humiliated and in no way surprised.

3:10 pm: I sit with a group of Heterosexual Females and dis-cuss our mutual feelings on Channing Tatum,* which for the record are quite positive. One female lends me a copy of *Glamour* and I read an article on "Fifty Ways to Have Sexy Summer Hair," which, as it turns out, is not all *that* hard, ladies.

3:30 pm: The presence of a water gun surprises me. Every time my female friends or I happen to doze off, the Heterosexual Males shoot us with ice-cold streams of water. It's like getting peed on by the Abominable Snowman every time I close my eyes. But less fun.

3:53 pm: I have just learned that Miller High Life is considered the "Champagne" of Bottled Beers.

4:00 pm–5:45 pm: I am asleep because of all the "champagne" that I've drunk.

6:00 pm: I begin to notice that any time I don't have something to say, I can just quote a line from *Anchorman* and the Heterosexual Males will literally fall to the ground laughing. I will repeat this technique eight more times before ending my wonderful day at the beach.

*My boyfriend saw Channing Tatum in a restaurant a few days ago. Totally unrelated, but I got so excited that I wanted to share.

The Heterosexual SAT #2:
Sentence Completions

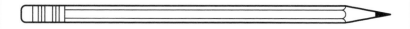

Uh-oh! It's time for another pop quiz! I'm sorry. I can assure you that I don't like writing them just as much as you don't like taking them. But you know what? Life is full of stuff you don't want to do but end up having to do. How do you think Hillary Clinton felt about being Secretary of State?

For this test, you'll be answering sentence completion questions.

EXAMPLE:

Jeffery Self smells so great they should:
A. Ask him to leave.
B. Ask him to shower.
C. Bottle him.
D. Start calling him Elizabeth Taylor.

Answer: While the obvious answer here is C, I would accept D, but only because it makes me feel really good about myself. Think you've got the hang of it? Good. Let's go!

1. Ever since I arrived in Las Vegas, I keep seeing _____.
   A. Priests
   B. Maps for New York
   C. Puppies
   D. Obese people with tickets to go see Elton John

2. I recently went to the beach with some Heterosexuals and got drunk playing _____ all day.
   A. Scrabble
   B. Beer Pong
   C. Barry Manilow Trivia
   D. Simpsons Monopoly

3. New York City is so beautiful this time of year; if only it didn't smell so much like _____.
   A. My dad after a jog
   B. Coconut shampoo
   C. Toothpaste
   D. Stale urine and broken dreams

4. My parents and I are going to Colonial Williamsburg this summer to learn about how _____ used to live.
   A. Aliens
   B. Cave people
   C. Our ancestors
   D. Angela Lansbury

5. Disney World was so crowded that we didn't get to ride
_____.
   A. Our bicycles
   B. The waves
   C. Splash Mountain
   D. Pierce Brosnan

6. I've only been to Cancun for Spring Break on one occasion,
and I left with a hickey and _____.
   A. A scholarship to Duke University
   B. Strep throat
   C. $1,000
   D. A really unfortunate evening caught on tape by *Girls
Gone Wild*

7. When going to the beach, it is important to wear _____.
   A. A dress shirt
   B. Sunscreen
   C. A feather boa and a wig you don't mind getting wet
   D. A belt and nothing else

8. John Mayer has slept with so many women they should
change his name to _____.
   A. John Mayor of Lady Town
   B. John Lay-her
   C. I'm not going to get any further with this one
because those first two are just too damn good. I'm
so clever.

9. While in Daytona Beach, my girlfriend won a wet _____ contest.
   A. Swimsuit
   B. Blanket
   C. T-shirt
   D. Willy

10. When migrating with a Heterosexual Male, it is likely he will refuse to ask for _____.
    A. A pee break
    B. A candy bar
    C. Directions
    D. Me to sing the entire soundtrack to *Dreamgirls*, but I will do it anyway

ANSWERS:

1. D; 2. B; 3. D; 4. C; 5. C; 6. D; 7. B; 8. Every answer is correct; 9. C; 10. C

Chapter 5

Heterosexual
Feeding Habits

HETEROSEXUALS, LIKE ALL OTHER MEMBERS OF THE ANIMAL kingdom, love to eat. But the only difference is that Heterosexuals *really* love to eat. I'm talking *eat*. E.A.T. All-you-can-eat-baby-backribs-at-Chili's-with-two-pitchers-of-margaritas-and-a-pound-of-bean-dip kind of eat.

Ever heard of Thanksgiving? It's my favorite holiday and guess what? It comes from the genius minds of Heterosexuals. Why? To give thanks and all that crap, but more importantly to eat more in one meal than one human being should eat in the entire month of November. Heterosexuals have done the same thing with Christmas and the Fourth of July. Basically any holiday where you spend all day eating and celebrating is because of Heterosexuals. So the next time you spot a Heterosexual, remember to say thank-you.

It's not just the holidays that the Heterosexuals have turned into food feasts; Heterosexuals are the people who thought up all-you-can-eat buffets, bottomless salads and breadsticks at

Olive Garden, and cake pops (for the Heterosexual on the go who loves cake, but is too busy to spend all that time slicing a piece, finding a fork, and consuming all that icing).

They even created an entire TV channel called the Food Network where, no matter what time of day you turn it on, there is always a British gay guy or a heavyset woman telling you about some sort of delicious food treat that is meant to make the mouths of Heterosexuals water. The Food Network is the closest thing to porn that the giant fat guy from *Lost* is going to get.

Before we begin exploring the feeding patterns of the Heterosexual, it is important to understand that not *all* Heterosexuals enjoy an evening spent eating the kind of greasy food that requires a bib, two Zantacs, and a stent put in one's heart. Far from it, the feeding patterns of Heterosexuals are as wide a variety as the T-shirt colors sold at American Apparel, but if you ask me, there's nothing more annoying than a Heterosexual health nut.

However, I'm getting ahead of myself. Within the Heterosexual community, there are both carnivores and herbivores, and everything in between. I grew up in a carnivorous household, as my dad worked and still works in the poultry industry. My dad is fine with my being an internationally beloved gay icon of stage and screen, he's fine with his hippie daughter, and he's fine with both of us being bleeding-heart liberals, but I think if either one of us came home and announced we had become vegetarians, he'd literally fall over dead, or at the very least politely ask us to leave and never come back.

Many Heterosexuals, both carnivores and herbivores alike, consider themselves *foodies*, a term created by Heterosexuals with no real hobbies to speak of other than eating. Calling themselves *foodies* gives them an excuse to spend $400 for a dinner consisting of foods they can't pronounce.

The following 10 food items are the most popular among the Heterosexual species, other than birthday cake, but everybody loves birthday cake (except for people who prefer pie and Jehovah's Witnesses). If you come into contact with a hungry Heterosexual, provide him/her with one of the dishes on the next page.

The Top 10 Most Popular Heterosexual Foods

1. **Their mom's recipe for spaghetti sauce:** Even when Heterosexuals aren't Italian, they always swear their mom's spaghetti sauce is the best there is. However, I hate to break it to you, but my mom's is the best—and I'm not even a Heterosexual.

2. **Soul Food (a.k.a. food made famous and delicious by black people):** Heterosexuals *love* to drive to parts of their towns they normally don't go to and eat deliciously greasy foods cooked up by some of the greatest African-American cooks in the country whom no one will ever hear of until somebody gives them a reality show.

3. **Potatoes:** Whether fried or baked, we all know Heterosexuals *love* potatoes. (Just look at what happened to them in Ireland during the Great Potato Famine. Spoiler alert: It was *not* good.)

4. **Coconut water:** Ever since Rihanna started telling Heterosexuals to drink coconut water, they simply can't stop, which marks the first and only time Heterosexuals will ever do what Rihanna tells them to do.

5. **Hot wings:** I'll get into this in just a little bit, but it is too important not to mention more than once.

6. **Popsicles:** Everyone's parents keep them in the house, but no one's parents *ever* comment on how suggestive it is to watch someone actually eat one. And so it should always remain.

7. **Chinese takeout:** Based solely on what I've seen in movies and TV, Heterosexuals *always* eat Chinese takeout on the floor of their new homes any time they move into new houses or apartments. Think about every scene where a Heterosexual has just moved into a new place in any movie in the history of time, and then you will understand exactly what I'm talking about.

8. **Pizza:** Most commonly eaten in the middle of the night when Heterosexuals are too intoxicated to remember.

9. **Hot dogs:** Whether it's at a baseball game, in someone's backyard BBQ, or at a Nathan's in their local mall, no Heterosexual carnivore can turn down a delicious hot dog. Or its cousin, the corn dog, which is just a hot dog dipped in batter and fried to a crisp. When I was a kid, I used to tell my peers that my dad invented the breakfast corn dog (a link sausage dipped in pancake batter and fried), but this was just a lie that didn't succeed in helping me become popular.

10. **And finally (and most importantly) Oreos:** Arguably the greatest thing to come from Heterosexuals since Levi blue jeans or Brad Pitt's abs in *Fight Club*. Hey, I said *arguably*.

Heterosexual Carnivores

The high sales of meat, the existence of heart disease, what my poultry-obsessed father has told me, and scientific studies all show that the majority of Heterosexuals are carnivorous creatures. These Heterosexuals enjoy the lush tastes of chicken, beef, pork, and, if the Heterosexual eats at expensive restaurants and/or is Chinese, duck. Here are some of the most popular dishes among Heterosexual Carnivores.

Cheeseburgers

Who doesn't love a cheeseburger? Well, Alicia Silverstone,* for one, but that's because she's a communist (just kidding; she's just annoying *and* a vegan, but we'll get to that later). It is a proven fact that nothing makes a Heterosexual Male feel more like a man than grilling these delicious beef patties in the backyard on a hot summer day. Popular among Frat Boys (page 47), Married Couples (page 38), and the actor John Goodman.

---

*Alicia Silverstone is a Heterosexual who was quite famous in the mid-1990s after starring in the successful comedy *Clueless*. She was *great* in this movie and went on to have a successful film career, but around the time that she started talking about natural childbirth on every talk show she went on, her career sort of peaked and now she mostly pops up at antifur fund-raisers and anywhere that supports public breast-feeding. By the way, why the hell haven't they made a *Clueless 2* yet?! It is still not too late, Hollywood insiders!

Jerky

Quite possibly the most Heterosexual of all foods, jerky is a deliciously lean meat, cut into strips, and then dried to prevent spoilage. One could argue that jerky is simply meat after undergoing an autopsy, however, I beg to differ. Jerky is one of my favorite snacks and can be prepared with beef, pork, chicken, and even deer meat. One Christmas, my cousin Hal was really excited because he'd gotten a jerky machine from Santa; I was equally excited, but because Santa had brought me a VHS copy of Stephen Sondheim's *Into the Woods* and a 100 percent Lycra Elvis costume and wig. Guess which one of us grew up to be a Heterosexual?

Bacon

If you've woken up in a Heterosexual's house on a Saturday morning, then, first of all, how did you get there and are you OK?! And second of all, you've probably smelled bacon. Heterosexuals have a ritual within their feeding pattern that if they're at home on a Saturday morning, they will without a doubt make bacon in a skillet while they watch Saturday morning cartoons. I can't explain why; I can only say I approve.

Appetizer Sampler

If you've ever had dinner with a Heterosexual at a chain restaurant such as Applebee's or Chili's, then you've undoubtedly enjoyed an appetizer sampler. This dish, created by food-loving Heterosexuals, is a platter of delicious pre-entrée treats, such as fried chicken wings, French fries, egg rolls, fried wontons, and one of the most impressive Heterosexual inventions to date: the mozzarella stick. Leave it to the Heterosexuals to come up with frying cheese. *Brilliant.* Speaking of cheese . . .

Nachos

Now, you might be questioning my inclusion of this in the carnivorous category, however, no self-respecting Heterosexual has ever ordered nachos without adding beef or chicken. Nachos are a great Heterosexual food because you can whip them up in a hurry. Say you open your front door to find three of your closest straight friends having arrived unannounced. Whip up some nachos and open a couple cans of whatever beer your dad left in your fridge when he was visiting last December, then sit back as the Heterosexuals enjoy.

Chicken Potpie

Have you ever had chicken potpie made by anyone other than a Straight Person? I didn't think so.

Gravy

Gravy is a gooey sauce that is either brown or off-white. I'm including that here because it is usually served on top of a meat (and sometimes biscuits). I am not sure where gravy comes from, and, to be honest, I don't think I want to. Mainly because it's something I've enjoyed for so long and something I can only assume is 1,000 percent terrible for me. That said, most

Heterosexuals would eat an armchair if you covered it in gravy, but don't actually try that because then you won't have an armchair.

Chili

Chili is a very competitive food among Heterosexuals. All Heterosexuals have their own recipe, and all of them swear that theirs is the best. I'm fairly partial to the chili at Wendy's, which is a dead giveaway that I don't know much about chili, which is a dead giveaway that I'm not a Heterosexual, which (and this isn't even related but it's worth mentioning) is a dead giveaway that I saw the movie *Mamma Mia* in theaters. Twice. And I liked it. I liked it all, y'all. Chili is such a popular Heterosexual dish that entire competitions are held to determine whose recipe is the best. This type of Heterosexual event is called a chili cook-off.*

Crock-Pots

This isn't a specific kind of food; however, Heterosexuals *love* cooking their meat in Crock-Pots, electric devices that slowly cook meat to juicy perfection. When asked why they love

---

*A chili cook-off is a daylong cookout where numerous teams compete to prove that they have the best chili recipe there is. My dad and I used to go to the chili cook-off in my hometown together. A lot of people would camp out, but we neverdid, most likely because any time my dad mentioned camping, I assumed he meant my performing a Bette Davis impersonation. We'd always attend the competition and sample all the entries, leaving with historically bad gas and stomachs that still haven't started feeling right again.

Crock-Pots, Heterosexuals will *always* reply, "It does all the work, and when I come home my house smells like roast beef!" Heterosexuals are one of the only species on planet Earth who desire a home that smells of roast beef.

Meat Loaf

Meat *and* carbs!!!

Hot Wings

Heterosexuals *love* these spicy, insanely messy to eat, delicious wings of small chickens. Especially when dipped in ranch dressing. These treats are usually served with a side of celery sticks that, when being served to a Heterosexual, will never be touched. I recently went out for wings with a Heterosexual Male I know, and when I reached for one of the celery sticks on the side of our wings basket, he looked at me as if I'd just whipped my penis out at a church picnic, then watched me, lost in thought, and said, "Hmm. I've just never seen anyone actually eat those before."

Heterosexual Herbivores

Heterosexual Herbivores are a vastly different group within the species. These meat-free Heterosexuals tend to enjoy things like yoga, independent film, folk art portraits of Bob Dylan, and wearing the organic cotton clothing sold on racks next to those weird massage chairs by the condiment table at Whole Foods.

Oftentimes, Heterosexual Herbivores can be a little too boastful about their vegetarian lifestyle. The really aggressive types are usually members of the Raw Food Movement, which is when you only eat foods that are uncooked and raw. I'm all for healthy living (I own running shoes, or, rather, my boyfriend does, and they happen to fit me, too), but I think that the Raw Food Movement is taking things just a little too far. But then again, who am I to judge? I made a sandwich out of stale graham crackers, grape jelly, and wasabi peas at 3 in the morning a few nights ago.

Here are some commonly enjoyed dishes among Heterosexual Herbivores.

Kale

Kale is the "in" food of the moment. It was all about pomegranates a few years ago, and for a brief period it was beets in the early 21st century, but nowadays it's all hail kale!* Kale is

*The All Hail Kale is an actual salad sold at Veggie Grill in Los Angeles—which is a fabulous place to spot famous Heterosexual Herbivores like Casey Affleck, Avril Lavigne, and Candice Bergen.

a leafy green that is known for being extremely healthy and is recommended by all sorts of health officials and talking heads. Heterosexual Herbivores go nuts for this kind of thing, and, in turn, kale has become as popular among Heterosexuals as spinach once was with Popeye. But I think it's safe to say that if Popeye were alive today, not only would he be under some *intense* investigation for steroid use, but he'd also totally trade in his can of spinach for a nice plate of kale. Oh, and Olive Oyl would *totally* be a lesbian.

Peanut Butter

If Jif Peanut Butter's slogan is any indication, Choosy Moms always choose Jif Peanut Butter for their Heterosexual families. And if the six months I spent in college are any indication, 20-somethings who smoke far too much pot choose it, too.

Gluten-Free Pancakes

Most Heterosexual Herbivores hate gluten as much as Mario Lopez hates carbs. What is gluten?, you may ask. It comes from wheat and is found in many, many foods. No one really talked about it until a few years ago when literally overnight just about half the people I know announced they were allergic to gluten and could only eat gluten-free things from now on. I'm sure some people *are* allergic to gluten, but it definitely seems like the kind of thing people merely claim to be allergic to because they don't like it. The way a lot of people do with mayonnaise by saying, "No mayo on the sandwich, I'm allergic" or the way I do with Nicki Minaj's music by saying, "No Nicki Minaj, I'm allergic."

Overpriced Cupcakes
Heterosexuals *love* to spend way too much money on cupcakes, and, honestly, who can blame them? Nothing says living like waiting in line for 10 minutes to pay $10 for a cupcake the size of a tennis ball. But a very, very delicious tennis ball.

Jasmine Rice
Jasmine rice is basically like any other rice except that it includes the word *jasmine* in its name. Heterosexuals enjoy requesting this rice at dinner to let their waiter know they are both worldly and a fan of Disney's *Aladdin*.

Grilled Cheese
Nothing says comfort to the Heterosexual like a grilled cheese sandwich. Add in a bowl of thick, creamy tomato soup for dipping, and the Heterosexual in question will roll over and let you rub his or her belly. Does anyone know if Justin Timberlake likes grilled cheese, and, if so, what's his address?

Egg Salad
I love almost all Heterosexual foods, but I draw the line at egg salad. Those two words together make my stomach turn. I like eggs and I like salad, but the two together sound pretty lethal to me. Heterosexuals, however, *love* egg salad, and enjoy making

it for picnics and cookouts. My least favorite kind of cookout is when the only side options are egg salad or one of its ugly cousins, such as potato salad, pasta salad, or tuna salad. Sure, they use the word *salad* in their names, but all these dishes are just whatever the first word is, mixed with mayonnaise, and, to me, that is a criminal offense. The same thing goes for . . .

Coleslaw

Even the name bothers me, because you think it's going to be coldslaw, but it's not, it's *cole*slaw. I have a friend named Cole and I love him, but I'll be honest with you: It took some effort to get past his name reminding me of coleslaw. *Slaw* in and of itself is a pretty nasty word, too. You can imagine a world in which the term *slaw* could be used to describe any number of disgusting bodily functions. Instead, however, it is a side dish made from shredded veggies, and once mixed with the ever-popular mayonnaise, is called coleslaw, which makes about as much sense to me as if they called it shop doo wop pow wow *zing*!

Chefs Heterosexuals Love

Heterosexuals love food so much that they've made celebrities out of some of the best Heterosexual chefs in the business. These food icons have entire empires constructed of television shows, cookbooks, and popular food blogs. Many of them come from the aforementioned Food Network (page 156), but the food TV craze doesn't stop there. These professional chefs have left an undeniable impact on the feeding patterns of all Heterosexuals:

Julia Child

Not just the basis for a really enjoyable Meryl Streep movie–*God, I love that movie! Don't you?*–however, Julia Child was one of the first television food superstars, the original Iron Chef. She taught Heterosexuals how to cook deliciously classy French cuisine. Also, totally unrelated: She was like two inches taller than almost every actor then working in Hollywood.

Paula Deen

I love Paula Deen. She is best known for her adorable Southern charm and mouth-watering comfort food, and has made billions out of saying, "Now you're gonna need half a cup of butter and half a cup of oil, y'all" 95 times a day. She hosts television shows, writes best-selling cookbooks, owns a line of cookware, and was even in a movie with Orlando Bloom a while back. However, before you get too excited, I'm legally obligated to mention that Kirsten Dunst was in that movie as well, and also Paula Deen has been diagnosed as diabetic. Sorry to ruin your day.

Guy Fieri

A Heterosexual Male who looks something like Paula Deen with a goatee. Known for his cooking shows and his unique trademark of wearing sunglasses on the back of his head for absolutely no reason whatsoever, Guy is all about hypermasculine food and energy, which leads many Heterosexual Watchers like myself to wonder just how small his penis really is.

Martha Stewart

First of all, I wish she were president. Second of all, she is a Heterosexual food mogul who cooks vastly different things than Guy or Paula. Martha Stewart caters to the Heterosexual who wishes to throw the classiest of Thanksgiving dinners or an elegant candlelit dinner party using things found in the Martha Stewart Home Collection at Kmart. Martha also went to prison for insider stock trading a few years back, and even worse, was played by Cybill Shepherd in not one but *two* made-for-TV movies.

Granny Smith

A world-famous Heterosexual known for being both a grandmother and a purveyor of apples.

Rachael Ray*

Somehow she's extremely popular, however, I've never met anyone who actually enjoys her. Rachael Ray spends every morning teaching Heterosexuals how to cook meals in 30 minutes, making her extremely popular among busy moms and fugitives on the run.

Top Chef

Many Metropolitan Heterosexuals consider *Top Chef* to be the greatest show in television history, and they just might be right. *Top Chef* has made chefs famous the same way *Keeping Up with the Kardashians* has made Kim Kardashian famous. Except that no one on *Top Chef* has made a sex tape, and I suspect Kim Kardashian has never even been inside a kitchen.

Now most Heterosexuals are *not* celebrity chefs and instead are forced to come up with meals with whatever they have lying around or whatever was on sale at the grocery store. These Heterosexuals represent everyman's pursuit of making a delicious meal out of a bottle of mustard and a box of noodles. Exploring a Heterosexual's refrigerator can tell you a lot about said Heterosexual's feeding patterns and the Heterosexual him- or herself. Check this out:

....

*I listened to a podcast once where Rachael Ray admitted to drinking a bottle of wine all by herself every night and then "just running it off on the treadmill" the next morning before hosting her live television show. My kind of girl.

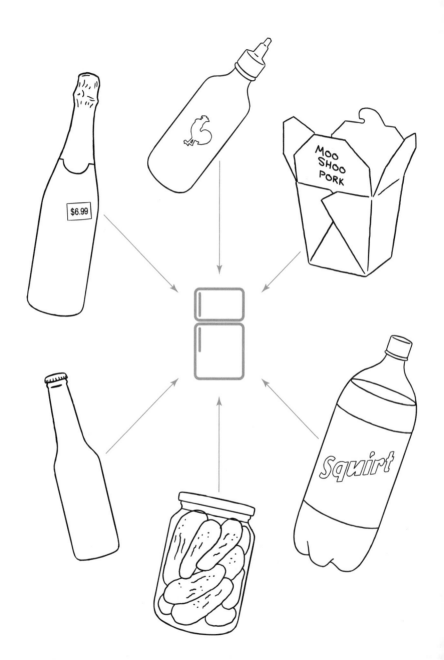

I have arrived in the Heterosexual Male's kitchen, and before I can even say hello, he offers me a beer, which I decline because it is 10 in the morning on a Monday.

Let's begin with the door. I see magnetized bottle openers (including one that plays the theme song to *The Dukes of Hazzard*), one of those create-a-sentence magnet sets, which our Heterosexual Male has used to spell out the phrase *take a dump with love Jim*, surrounded by unpaid parking tickets, a Christmas card with someone's baby on it, a handwritten reminder to "Call Back Alicia from that Mexican Restaurant in the Valley," and a calendar from 2009.

Things inside the fridge include:

- A take-out container marked *Moo Shoo Pork*, on which the Heterosexual Male has written "Throw out by Friday." Today is Monday.

- An entire drawer of Coors Light.

- One empty bottle of I Can't Believe It's Not Butter Spray, which I am told *not* to throw away.

- A bottle of champagne with a price sticker marked $6.99, which the Heterosexual Male tells me he's saving for a special occasion.

- A jar of pickles, which the Heterosexual Male opens and eats from three times in the short period that I'm there.

- A bottle of Sriracha, which the Heterosexual Male claims he puts on everything from waffles to spaghetti.

- A liter bottle of a soda I've never tried in my life called Squirt, which might be the most disgusting soda name I can come up with next to Straight-Up Urine in a Bottle.

- In this particular refrigerator, I discover a shelf that is common in refrigerators owned by Heterosexual Males, and that is the *very* important Girlfriend Shelf.

What Is the Girlfriend Shelf?

As we all know, Heterosexual Males and Females can be very different. (Remember *Dharma and Greg*? Really? OK. Well, you didn't miss much.) Everything from hygiene to feeding patterns is different between the two sexes, and, oftentimes, when a Heterosexual Male and Female who are in a relationship where the two involved parties do not live together, the Heterosexual Female stakes out a designated area within the Heterosexual Male's home called the Girlfriend Shelf.

In a Heterosexual Male's home, you are likely to find more than one Girlfriend Shelf; in fact, sometimes you can find up to three Girlfriend Shelves in one household. They are:

The Bedroom Girlfriend Shelf: Also known (in some subcultures) as the Bedroom Girlfriend Drawer. On this shelf (or in this drawer), the Heterosexual Female will usually keep a handful of personal clothing items, including a couple pairs of underwear, socks, a comfortable T-shirt to watch television in, and an extra pair of jeans, as well as something nice enough to wear to brunch if she ends up sleeping over on a Friday and forgets to bring a spare dress. The Heterosexual Female will create a micro version of her own closet, staking out her ground, and, if you ask me, taking a bold risk by leaving a pair of $200 jeans in the same apartment as a guy who owns every single season of *Power Rangers* on DVD.

The Bathroom Girlfriend Shelf: Found inside the shower or medicine cabinet, this shelf houses all the Heterosexual Female's hygiene products, including shampoo, conditioner (the Heterosexual Male will only be able to provide the bottle of shampoo-and-conditioner-in-one that he purchased at the dollar store), lady soap (beyond my realm of expertise, but ladies tend to smell really nice: Good job, ladies!), Midol, tampons, and lady deodorant. (This is totally unrelated, but I've been using women's Dove deodorant since high school and literally didn't realize it was for women until about three months ago—which still hasn't stopped me from using it, by the way.)

And the aforementioned:

Refrigerator Girlfriend Shelf: On this shelf, the Heterosexual Female will keep the food she likes to eat, but that the Heterosexual Male never thinks to buy—things like fresh fruit, individual packets of cream cheese, a bottle of white wine, and a six-pack of that Activia yogurt that makes Jamie Lee Curtis so excited about pooping on TV commercials all the time.

Before we move on, it is pop quiz time! I'll bet you thought I forgot, didn't you? Well, then, you don't know me at all!

The Heterosexual SAT #3:
True or False

This round of our Heterosexual SAT will be True or False. Please answer the questions truthfully, then consult the answer guide to see how you did before moving on.

EXAMPLE:

American Horror Story and *Nashville* star Connie Britton is most known for her one-woman show about vampires called *Connie Bitten*.
○ True
○ False

Answer: False

1. The term *foodies* is used to describe a group of sexually liberated Heterosexuals who enjoy using food during sexual activities.
   ○ True
   ○ False

2. The appetizer samplers that Heterosexuals enjoy in chain restaurants always include a pack of chewing gum and a pair of edible panties.
   ○ True
   ○ False

3. Country superstar Carrie Underwood doesn't just have the voice of an angel and legs for literally days, she is also a Heterosexual Herbivore.
   ○ True
   ○ False

4. My father is so obsessed with raw food that he won't even walk by a grocery store, because he can smell the pesticides and ovens.
   ○ True
   ○ False

5. My mom does a lot of shopping at Chico's.
   ○ True
   ○ False

6. Jerky is the state fruit of Alabama.
   ○ True
   ○ False

7. Paula Deen should run for president.
   ○ True
   ○ False
   (Before you answer this one, think about how much fun those debates would be.)

8. I, Jeffery Self, find Heterosexual Herbivore Alicia Silverstone to be a bit much.
   ○ True
   ○ False

9. *Marley and Me* is a documentary about Bob Marley and Mimi Rogers.
   ○ True
   ○ False

10. Kale is so "in" that Hipsters have started to resent it.
    ○ True
    ○ False

Chapter 6

Heterosexual Culture

WHILE ONLY A SELECT NUMBER OF HETEROSEXUALS ENJOY THE musical styling of country music singer Martina McBride, *all* Heterosexuals agree on many of the same things. For example, *all* Heterosexuals have seen the James Cameron movie *Titanic*, and if you ever come across a Heterosexual who claims he hasn't, then he's either lying or has suffered a serious case of amnesia, in which case, call 9-1-1 before it turns into a situation like the movie *Fifty First Dates* starring Drew Barrymore and Adam Sandler, a movie about a guy who falls in love with a girl who has suffered amnesia, and every time they hang out he's forced to make her fall in love with him all over again. If there's one thing more exhausting than Drew Barrymore, it is Drew Barrymore playing someone who can't remember anyone she knows, where she's from, or how to open a can of SpaghettiOs.

Considering that *all* Heterosexuals have seen *Titanic*, take a look at this graph chronicling how they feel about the Academy Award–winning super hit that made Leonardo DiCaprio the fantasy of all teenage girls for most of the late 1990s. Or rather, until Ryan Phillippe came around.

How Heterosexuals Feel about *Titanic*

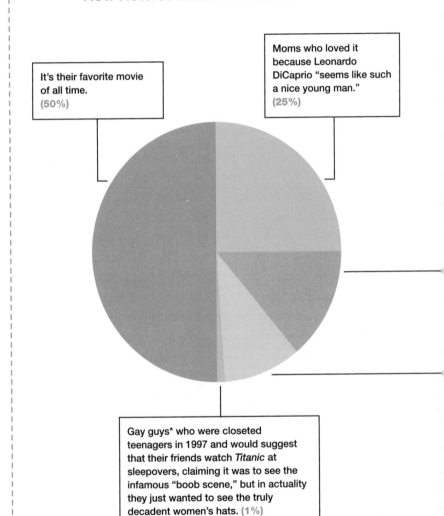

It's their favorite movie of all time.
(50%)

Moms who loved it because Leonardo DiCaprio "seems like such a nice young man."
(25%)

Gay guys* who were closeted teenagers in 1997 and would suggest that their friends watch *Titanic* at sleepovers, claiming it was to see the infamous "boob scene," but in actuality they just wanted to see the truly decadent women's hats. **(1%)**

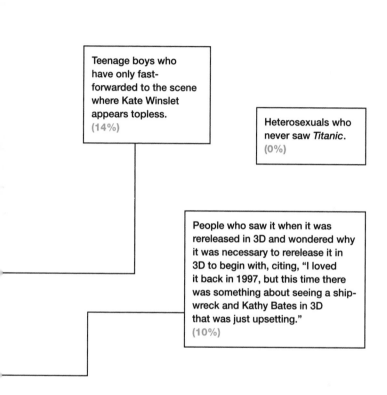

Teenage boys who have only fast-forwarded to the scene where Kate Winslet appears topless.
(14%)

Heterosexuals who never saw *Titanic*.
(0%)

People who saw it when it was rereleased in 3D and wondered why it was necessary to rerelease it in 3D to begin with, citing, "I loved it back in 1997, but this time there was something about seeing a ship-wreck and Kathy Bates in 3D that was just upsetting."
(10%)

You see, while many Heterosexuals have their own take on *Titanic*, they've all seen it, and they all feel *something*. Let's take a look at another popular film that any self-respecting Heterosexual is required to see.

*I make up this 1%.

Heterosexuals Who Have Seen
The Notebook and Why

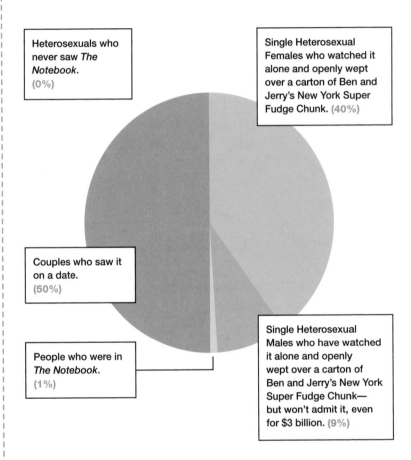

Heterosexuals who never saw *The Notebook*. (0%)

Single Heterosexual Females who watched it alone and openly wept over a carton of Ben and Jerry's New York Super Fudge Chunk. (40%)

Couples who saw it on a date. (50%)

People who were in *The Notebook*. (1%)

Single Heterosexual Males who have watched it alone and openly wept over a carton of Ben and Jerry's New York Super Fudge Chunk—but won't admit it, even for $3 billion. (9%)

Pretty interesting stuff, huh? Well, here's one more that is slightly different.

Heterosexuals Who Have Seen *Burlesque* and Why

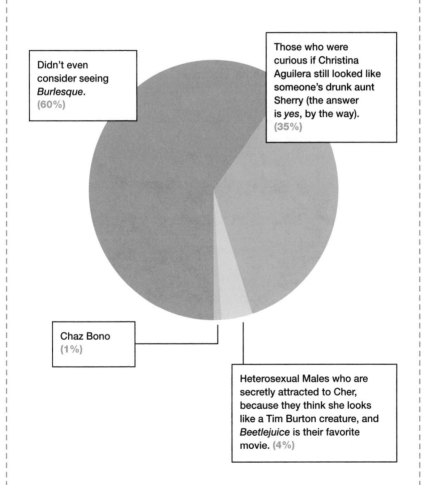

Didn't even consider seeing *Burlesque*. (60%)

Those who were curious if Christina Aguilera still looked like someone's drunk aunt Sherry (the answer is *yes*, by the way). (35%)

Chaz Bono (1%)

Heterosexual Males who are secretly attracted to Cher, because they think she looks like a Tim Burton creature, and *Beetlejuice* is their favorite movie. (4%)

See how that works? In the case of *Titanic* and *The Notebook,* you've got a movie specifically made for Heterosexuals, and in the case of *Burlesque,* you've got a movie made for an extremely small portion of Heterosexuals and drag queens who have grown tired after having watched their DVD of *Showgirls** 500 times.

While we're on the topic of Heterosexual cinema, a *fantastic* way to learn about Heterosexuals is from their Netflix movie queues.

---

*Fun fact about *Showgirls* star Elizabeth Berkley, whom we also know and love from *Saved by the Bell*. Just about every day in Los Angeles, you can drive by the same café on Melrose in West Hollywood and spot Elizabeth in full hair and makeup sitting at a laptop. One assumes she's either writing, or simply displaying herself to passing Homosexuals as her own form of community service. Either way, we all appreciate it.

Heterosexuals and Movies

What a person watches can tell you *a lot* about whose team they're batting for. Here are some movie titles that should serve as immediate red flags that you've spotted a Heterosexual.

Marley and Me
A heartwarming tale of when Heterosexuals get a dog and have kids. Spoiler alert: One of the title characters dies, and it's not Me.

Bride Wars
An underrated comedy starring Goldie Hawn's daughter and the girl who isn't Meryl Streep in *The Devil Wears Prada*.

Cast Away
What can I say? For Heterosexuals, it goes: God, Tom Hanks,* and the President of the United States—in that order of importance. Also, Helen Hunt is in this, and Heterosexuals *love* her. Or rather, they did in the mid-1990s.

The Bridges of Madison County
Middle-aged Heterosexuals have sex and look at old bridges! It is, without a doubt, your mom's favorite movie.

....

*Tom Hanks is the greatest actor in the history of all Heterosexual Cinema, and I will fight *anyone* who wants to argue otherwise. *You got that, Robert Downey Jr.?!*

The Lord of the Rings

Heterosexuals love a reason to line up for something in the middle of the night, and this series provided that for the nerdiest of Heterosexuals. I've never seen any of these movies, but only because they're *so* long. And unless Barbra Streisand is going to sing "I'm the Greatest Star," I'm not all that interested in sitting through a three-and-a-half-hour movie.

???

That movie where Julianne Moore plays the lady who makes pies in Ohio (can't remember the name and not going to look it up).

P.S. I Love You

Never seen it, but anytime I say something about not caring for Hilary Swank,* a Heterosexual friend will argue, "But what about *P.S. I Love You*?!"

---

*I suppose we've reached the point in the book when I need to address my lingering hostility toward Hilary Swank. It's obvious, but no one is acknowledging it, like how Coke Zero is actually better than original Coke, so at this point there's no reason to even sell original Coke. Hilary Swank simply rubs me the wrong way; I'm sorry, but she does. It also doesn't help that she's stolen *two* Academy Awards from the ever-deserving, great Annette Bening. I don't completely know what this has to do with Heterosexuals except that Hilary is famous and identifies as Heterosexual, though, I think it's safe to say we *all* have an eyebrow raised.

The Civil War: A Film by Ken Burns

Nobody likes to spend 10 hours with old people talking about the Civil War more than Heterosexuals and masochists.

Any and Every Adam Sandler Movie

Somebody is buying tickets to those movies, and it ain't me—or RuPaul.

27 Dresses*

This is a universally enjoyed movie, and one that represents a hopeful time in America before we realized what a monster Katherine Heigl is.

Forrest Gump

This movie manages to combine two of the things mentioned above that Heterosexuals love the most: Tom Hanks *and* the president. Oh! And oldies music! Heterosexuals *love* oldies music.

....

*Katherine Heigl was briefly one of the most prominently beloved movie stars of the Heterosexual species. The Heterosexual first became famous when she appeared on the television show *Grey's Anatomy*, a weekly hour of television that most Heterosexuals describe as "riveting," "beautiful," and "endlessly relatable." On that show, Katherine Heigl appeared as a sassy but gorgeous female doctor working in a fast-paced Seattle hospital. Things you can expect to hear Heterosexuals say about Katherine Heigl include: "She's just like my sister-in-law Pam." (Said by your office mate with the *Vampire Diaries* daily desk calendar.) "I think she's hot." (Said by someone's boyfriend.) "*27 Dresses* was like my biography!" (Said by Lisa, your alcoholic hairdresser cousin from Tampa, Florida.)

Heterosexuals and Music

Movies aren't the only cultural interest of Heterosexuals–far from it, in fact. Heterosexuals enjoy all sorts of television, writing, music, and art. I recently interviewed a Heterosexual Male at my local record store to find out more about Heterosexual music.

Me: Why is it that all Heterosexuals enjoy Kings of Leon?

Heterosexual: Well, have you ever listened to their music?

Me: No.

Heterosexual: They are awesome!

Me: OK, right. But who are they?

Heterosexual: They're a band; they write rock music; and it's really catchy.

Me: Are they actual kings?

Heterosexual: No.

Me: Are they from any sort of royal, aristocratic background?

Heterosexual: No. They're a band.

Me: Yes. From Leon. Which brings me to my other question: Where is Leon? And what kind of city is it?

Heterosexual: Leon isn't a city.

Me: Oh. So is it a country?

Heterosexual: No.

Me: Ah. It's a continent.

(The Heterosexual walks away.)

What did I learn from this conversation? Well, for one, that the Kings of Leon should actually be known as the Common Civilians of the Fictitious Leon, but also that you can't expect me to explain every single facet of the Heterosexual Lifestyle. Er, wait . . . that is the point of this book. Listen, these are the same people responsible for pajama jeans and Fergie, so just go with it.

Speaking of Fergie, celebrities are beloved among Heterosexuals, especially attractive ones. After all, Heterosexuals *are* human. Like any other species, all Heterosexuals have their ultimate celebrity crushes. For the record, my celebrity crushes are Matthew McConaughey and Suze Orman. (I obviously have a type.) However, mass surveys show the celebrities on the next pages are the most common celebrity crushes among Heterosexuals.

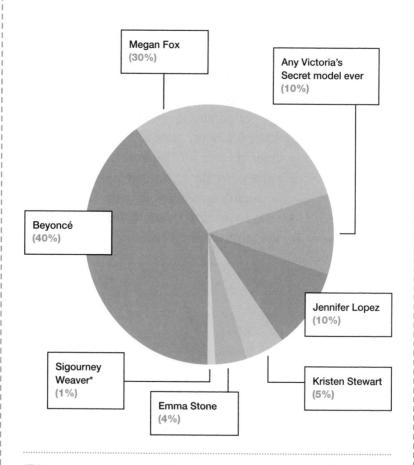

Celebrity Crushes
of the Heterosexual Male

Megan Fox
(30%)

Any Victoria's
Secret model ever
(10%)

Beyoncé
(40%)

Jennifer Lopez
(10%)

Sigourney
Weaver*
(1%)

Emma Stone
(4%)

Kristen Stewart
(5%)

*This percentage is made up of Sigourney Weaver's husband, Jim Simpson, and a handful of sci-fi nerds who have never seen a naked woman in real life and most likely never will.

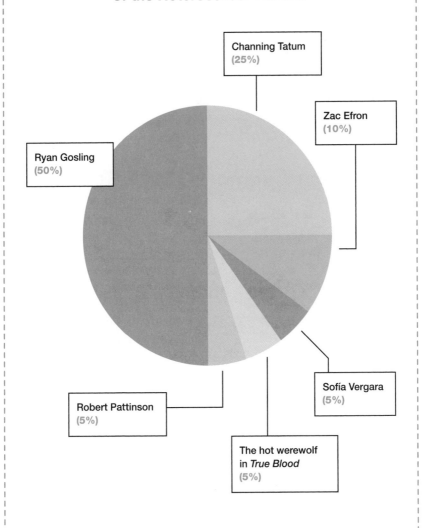

Celebrity Crushes
of the Heterosexual Female

Channing Tatum
(25%)

Zac Efron
(10%)

Ryan Gosling
(50%)

Sofía Vergara
(5%)

Robert Pattinson
(5%)

The hot werewolf
in *True Blood*
(5%)

Heterosexuals and Reading

I am constantly being asked the same question: "Can Heterosexuals read?" And my answer is always the same: "Except for Heidi Montag, and the character Precious based on the novel *Push* by Sapphire, yes, of course Heterosexuals can read." In fact, Heterosexuals are responsible for some of the most successful books of all time, like the extremely popular *Fifty Shades of Grey* series.

What Is *Fifty Shades of Grey*?

This is a trilogy chronicling an S&M relationship between two Heterosexuals that was originally written as fan fiction for another literary Heterosexual staple known as the *Twilight* series, which profiles a group of teenage vampires and werewolves who have a lot of sex for people their age. *Fifty Shades of Grey* takes readers on one woman's journey into sexual exploration, opening up Heterosexuals' eyes to the kind of shocking sexual adventure that Madonna calls "a Tuesday."

Why Is *Fifty Shades of Grey* So Popular Among Heterosexual Females?

The short answer is because it is something sexy to think about, but the long answer is much more complicated and would require me to tie you up and whip you, neither of which I'm prepared to do at this time. Sorry! I've got a mani/pedi appointment at two.

Of course, Heterosexuals read other novels besides *Fifty Shades of Grey*, just not in recent history. One thing that never changes, though, is the Heterosexual's passion for magazines. Heterosexuals love magazines, and a lot can be learned about the Heterosexual culture from the ones they read.

Playboy
Second to Hugh Hefner himself, *Playboy* is one of America's oldest and creepiest institutions.

Maxim
Playboy, without the boobs and franchise of hit reality television shows that I watch pretty much anytime I'm at home and awake.

People
No one likes to know where Kristen Stewart buys her smoothies more than Heterosexuals. Jamba Juice, by the way.

Men's Fitness
Unlike myself, Heterosexual Males actually use these 200 pages of gorgeous male bodies for . . . fitness.

O
Two words: Oprah Winfrey.

The New Yorker

Geared toward metropolitan Heterosexuals who read this while drinking delicious, overpriced espressos and looking down on the Midwest.

Martha Stewart Living

Mom porn.

Elle

Two hundred pages on the perfect summer top.

Details

This barely makes the list, as it is technically a magazine geared toward Metrosexuals, however, spend more than a minute with it, and you'll realize it's literally the gayest magazine since Neil Patrick Harris's monthly newsletter.*

Time

Where the Heterosexual goes to find out just how fucked up our world is on a week-to-week basis.

Sports Illustrated

To be perfectly honest, I have never even touched a copy of *Sports Illustrated*, but I assume it's about sports and possibly illustrations.

----

*Neil Patrick Harris doesn't have a monthly newsletter or, if he does, I'm not on his mailing list, which, to be honest, is a very likely possibility.

Rolling Stone
A platform for famous Heterosexual singers to make such regrettable statements as John Mayer's "I'd never have sex with a black woman."

Paper
Where Heterosexual Hipsters find out what they're supposed to be obsessed with this week.

The New York Times Book Review
Where readers can find a glowing review of this book that praises author Jeffery Self as the next Danielle Steel!*

Real Simple
For Heterosexuals who enjoy gay people telling them what to do with their home.

Seventeen
This magazine is full of teen heartthrob photos and is most popular among teenage Heterosexual Females. However, I'm fairly certain the first time my family suspected I was gay was when all six copies of *Seventeen* with Leonardo DiCaprio cover stories went missing from my sister's room and turned up hidden between my box spring and mattress.

---

*The reviewer didn't say that, as far as I know, but there's always a chance.

The Top 10 Modern Heterosexuals You Should Know

1. **Meryl Streep:** The most important Heterosexual of all time.

2. **Meryl Streep's mother:** The second most important Heterosexual of all time.

3. **Oprah:** Duh.

4. **Barack Obama:** He is the first African-American president, and he is also really good friends with Oprah! (See above.)

5. **Sarah Palin:** She was almost elected vice president of the United States, but more importantly is the only woman to have been played on television by both Tina Fey *and* Julianne Moore.

6. **Cap'n Crunch:** One of my personal favorite Heterosexuals.

7. **Tom Cruise:** Yeah, I know.

8. **The inventor of Nair:** Beloved by Heterosexual Females, as well as a very unique subset of Heterosexual Males, including both *Jersey Shore*'s The Situation and former California governor and all-around meathead Arnold Schwarzenegger.

9. **Julia Roberts:** She is and always will be the Heterosexual's Sweetheart.

10. **Sandra Bullock:** She is and always will be the Heterosexual's Other Sweetheart.

Famous Heterosexuals

Many of the world's most important people are Heterosexuals, but only a handful of Heterosexuals are the world's most important people. Kind of trippy to think about, huh?

Those last two names are considered Heterosexual Royalty and are arguably the most important women in history. They are esteemed and beloved icons within the Heterosexual community and the closest thing America has to princesses. At some point in their lives, every Heterosexual must answer the very difficult question: "Am I a Julia Roberts kind of Heterosexual or a Sandra Bullock kind of Heterosexual?"

As a rule, most Heterosexuals just innately know but, for some, this is one of the hardest decisions a Heterosexual will ever have to make. I, myself, have grappled with this question for years and have recently come to the conclusion that while I love Sandra, my heart belongs to Julia. Unless, of course, Sandra Bullock is reading this book, in which case, Julia who? *Call me, Sandy!* You're my gurl!

For Heterosexuals (or anyone else) who cannot decide, I've created this very easy-to-answer series of questions to help you or the Heterosexual in your life figure out this extremely pressing matter.

Julia or Sandra?
The Great Question of Our Time

1. When you first saw *Pretty Woman*, you thought:
   A. Who is this woman? She isn't all that pretty.
   B. This is the greatest romantic comedy I've ever seen.
   C. Maybe I want to be a prostitute.

   If you answered B, you are Team Julia. If you answered A, you are an asshole. And if you answered C, you should really think twice before you go down that road.

2. When you watched the scene where Julia Roberts dies in *Steel Magnolias*, you:
   A. Thought about someone you've lost, but then started thinking about what you wanted for dinner.
   B. Didn't cry.
   C. Threw yourself at the television and screamed, "Take me instead!!"

   If you answered C, you are without a doubt a Julia Roberts fan. If you answered A or B, you are a heartless monster.

3. When did you first hear about Sandra Bullock?
   A. *Speed.*
   B. *While You Were Sleeping.*
   C. When she won an Oscar for that movie about the giant black teenager.

Pretty much any of these answers make you Team Sandra. However, if you answered C, you're probably a racist. Just sayin'.

4. Your house is on fire, and you've already rescued all your valuables, sentimental items, and pets. You have one minute to run back in and grab one DVD off your shelf. Which do you choose?
   A. *Runaway Bride.*
   B. *The Proposal.*
   C. The Barbra Streisand remake of *A Star Is Born.*

If you answered A, you're Team Julia. If you answered B, you're Team Sandra. If you answered C, you're a Homosexual.

5. Which breakup broke your heart more?
   A. When Sandra's husband cheated on her with that woman covered in tattoos.
   B. Julia and Benjamin Bratt.
   C. Julia and Lyle Lovett.

This is pretty obvious. If you answered A, you're Team Sandra. If you answered B, you're Team Julia. If you answered C, you're out of your mind, because that was the weirdest relationship in the history of everything. Or you're Lyle Lovett.

Knowing whether the Heterosexuals you're dealing with are Team Julia or Team Sandra will help you better understand where they're coming from in all areas, from the economy to how they feel about that scene where Julia Roberts wears a fat suit in *America's Sweethearts*.

Recognizing Fictional Heterosexuals and Non-Heterosexuals

There are many fictional characters in pop culture that are thought to be Heterosexuals due to what we've been told by movies, books, our parents, and the liberal media. However, as with all potential Heterosexuals, their true orientation is always up for debate. Recognizing the Heterosexual and Non-Heterosexual traits in the fictional characters we all know and love can substantially strengthen your ability to spot the Heterosexuals in your own life. Also, pondering Cruella De Vil is just a nice way to spend any afternoon. Right, Glenn Close?

Ariel (a.k.a. the Little Mermaid)
This woman sacrificed her ability to breathe underwater and wear nothing but seashells over her breasts—*all* for a man. If she's not a Heterosexual, I don't know who is.

Smokey the Bear
If you've ever gone camping, you've probably pooped outside. Also, you've probably seen signs with photos of Smokey the Bear. We're asked to believe that he's a bear that somehow became a licensed forest ranger and can somehow always keep his hat on. If you can get past that (and you can if you try), you'll see that Smokey the Bear has *a lot* of Heterosexual qualities. For one, he *loves* being outdoors, which is a very common trait among Heterosexual Males, and also, he *loves* not wearing a

shirt while he does it. Have you ever seen a Heterosexual Male wandering through the woods *and* keeping his shirt on? No. I didn't think so. Smokey the Bear is as straight as an arrow; his counterpart, named Winnie, however, is a much different story.

Winnie the Pooh
Another bear, but much more delicate and sensitive. Winnie is not a Heterosexual, and I think that's as obvious as his addiction to honey, which is a real problem, by the way. None of his friends are addressing it, and I'm not calling Piglet an enabler, but I'm not *not* calling him an enabler, either. Y'know?

The Kool-Aid Man
This is a Heterosexual. How do I know? There is no gay male on planet Earth who would happily consume that many empty calories from a sugary drink without at the very least adding vodka.

Cruella De Vil
This is a gay guy in drag if I've ever seen one, and believe me, I've seen one!

Golem
This Tolkien character isn't a Heterosexual. How can I tell? He's clinically obsessed with jewelry and has one of the thinnest bodies I've seen on a male since everyone was posting those nude photos of Daniel Radcliffe on my Facebook wall. Speaking of which, why did y'all stop doing that?

Goofy

People have raised an eyebrow at this confirmed bachelor who's been suspiciously single for as long as I can remember, but I can attest firsthand that he is indeed a Heterosexual. I'm not going into details on how I know this; just trust me, based solely on the fact that I haven't been legally allowed into Disney World since 1992.

See how easy that is? Try it for yourself! Open up your favorite book, or turn on your favorite cartoon and hone your Heterosexual-Watching skills all from the comfort of your own home!

Ding-Dong! Who's there? Oh! It's another pop quiz!

The Heterosexual SAT #4:
Multiple Choice

In this pop quiz, you'll be answering questions related to chapters you've read thus far. I sure hope you've been paying attention, or else everyone you know will be extremely disappointed in you, starting first with me. Let's begin.

EXAMPLE:

For Christmas, it is tradition to decorate:
A. A pumpkin.
B. A tree.
C. A lady who could really benefit from having bangs.
D. The inside of your mouth with glitter.

Answer: B

1. Which one of these habitats did I *not* mention as a popular Heterosexual Habitat?
   A. Major metropolitan areas.
   B. Rural areas.
   C. Kevin Spacey's pool house.
   D. Suburbia.

2. How would you rate this author's writing style?
   A. Boring.
   B. Moderately entertaining.
   C. The worst ever.
   D. Scary, it was so good. Like really. I'm going to have to sleep with the lights on tonight.

3. Which one of these people is *not* a Heterosexual you should know?
   A. Julia Roberts.
   B. Sandra Bullock.
   C. The creator of *Mad About You.*
   D. Barack Obama.

4. Which one of these can you *not* do in the Heterosexual migration spot Las Vegas?
   A. See topless showgirls.
   B. Enjoy the musical styling of Shania Twain.
   C. Indulge in all-you-can-eat crab legs.
   D. Find anyone who has ever read *Wuthering Heights*.

5. Which one of these names sounds the least Heterosexual?
   A. Stacey.
   B. Rachel.
   C. Bart.
   D. Taylor Lautner.

6. Choosy Moms choose what?
   A. Juice.
   B. Jif.
   C. Gin.
   D. Jury duty.

7. Which one of these movies has every Heterosexual seen?
   A. *Bring It On Again.*
   B. *Titanic.*
   C. *Oogieloves in the Big Balloon Adventure.*
   D. *Hot Cowboy Studs III.*

8. If I were a Heterosexual Female, which one of these men would I want to marry?
   A. Ryan Gosling.
   B. Channing Tatum.
   C. Matthew McConaughey.
   D. Alexander Skarsgard.
   (Hint: There is no wrong answer.)

9. Who is the no. 1 most important Heterosexual alive today?
   A. The kid from *Boy Meets World.*
   B. Sherri Shepherd.
   C. Meryl Streep.
   D. Oprah.

10. Which one of these things is the appropriate thing to say to a Heterosexual Female after she's had a baby?
    A. "You look like John Travolta in *Hairspray*!"
    B. "Are you going to keep it?"
    C. "Your baby is the cutest thing I've ever seen!"
    D. "When was the last time you showered?"

ANSWERS:

1. C; 2. D; 3. C; 4. D; 5. D; 6. B; 7. B; 8. All answers are correct; 9. C; 10. C

Chapter 7

Heterosexual Calls

JUST LIKE BIRDS, DEER, WHALES, AND PEOPLE FROM THE SOUTH, Heterosexuals have very distinct communication patterns, and, oftentimes, in order to get a Heterosexual's attention, you will need to use the language and calls that are native to their species. Before we discuss the best ways to communicate with a Heterosexual, you must first understand their language itself. Use the following glossary as a reference point any time you're attempting to communicate with a Heterosexual.

The Heterosexual Glossary

Bro *noun.* A slang term that is short for *brother*, but does not mean one's *actual* brother. Heterosexuals are *very* capable people, frequently shortening key words in an effort to achieve verbal efficiency. However, the term *sis* is a lot less popular when referring to Heterosexual Females, and if you refer to a female as "sister," she will automatically assume that you think she's either (A) a nun or (B) a Sassy Black Lady (page 63). Not dissing either, by the way.

Cougar *noun.* A popular term given to Heterosexual Females of a certain age who enjoy the company of younger men. It should be noted that there is no comparable term for Heterosexual Males who do the same thing. Except maybe "that creep who looks like Mr. Belding from *Saved by the Bell* who is always trying to buy me drinks at the bar in the Roosevelt Hotel" or Donald Trump.

Diaper Genie *noun.* This one really threw me for a loop the first few times I heard it. I know what you're thinking, and before you say anything, *no*, a Diaper Genie is nothing like Robin Williams's character in *Aladdin*, nor does it have anything to do with the popular 1960s Barbara Eden sitcom *I Dream of Jeannie*. This Genie is a piece of equipment with no magical ability. However, it is beloved by Heterosexual parents for sealing a baby's dirty diapers so one's house doesn't smell like the Porta-Potties at Burning Man.

Divorce *noun.* Heterosexuals have the nationwide right to be legally married. It is a privilege that they do not take lightly; however, along with it comes the staggeringly popular process known as divorce. I am a child of divorce, by which I mean I was a kid when Brad Pitt divorced Jennifer Aniston for Angelina Jolie, and I have the emotional scars to prove it. In a divorce, assets are legally divided, alimony is paid, and if children are involved, parental rights become an issue. Divorce is one of the more heartbreaking experiences a Heterosexual might go through, next to the death of a beloved pet or vacationing in Arkansas.

Friends with Benefits *pl. noun.* The way a friends-with-benefits situation works is that two people, who happen to be friends, have a sexual relationship that does not stray from what happens between the sheets. These friends might go to baseball games together, attend the same game nights, and even cohost dual birthday parties, but no matter how romantic their friendship might seem on the surface, they are simply two Heterosexuals partaking in a consensual, strictly sexual relationship with no plans to alter it whatsoever.* It is similar to the relationship gay men have with everyone they know.

"Getting m'hair done" *verb.* With the exception of bald people and weirdos who grow their hair really long and work as bar wenches at renaissance fairs, all of us get our hair cut, but Heterosexual Females make the process a much bigger deal than anyone else. A Heterosexual

---

*Except, of course, when the Heterosexual Female inevitably falls head-over-heels in love with the Heterosexual Male. Happens every time.

Female plans her hair appointment *weeks* in advance, sometimes months, and, once there, the process can take upwards of three hours, leaving the males of the species to wander around the mall and try to find ways to kill three hours in the massage chairs at Brookstone.

Jerk *noun.* A term Heterosexual Females and I use to describe recording artist Chris Brown.

Kenny G *noun.* A popular musician within the Heterosexual community, this saxophone player has served as the soundtrack to many a Heterosexual romantic evening. Besides playing the saxophone, he's also known for having pretty much the exact same hairdo as Andie MacDowell.

MILF *noun.* A commonly used term of desire among Heterosexual Males who enjoy the company of slightly older females, preferably those raising families. MILF stands for "Mom I'd Like to Fuck," and I can confidently say it is a word I've never and doubt I will ever say out loud. Unless I end up recording an audio version of this book, in which case, you just listened to what I said and the previous statements hold no truth, plus, you're probably thinking I have a great speaking voice and wondering if I sing, too, in which case, thank you and yes. Noted MILFs include Jessica Simpson, Teri Hatcher, Elisabeth Hasselbeck, Gwen Stefani, Demi Moore, Heidi Klum, and my aunt Kay.

Minivan *noun.* Driven by both Heterosexual Parents and Heterosexual Perverts alike.

"M'truck" *noun.* A commonly used term among Heterosexual Males, referring to their form of transportation. When a Heterosexual Male drives a truck, he will never address it as "my green 2012 Ford F-150" or whatever other model it might be; he will always simply call it "m'truck."

Muddin' *verb.* This is a popular activity among Heterosexuals living in rural areas where one can visit vast tracts of land in m'truck, and drive around in circles, causing m'truck to slide all over the place and mud to go everywhere. The appeal of this activity has been argued by many in my field, but it makes Heterosexuals so darn happy that there's no chance it will be discontinued any time soon.

My Girlfriend *noun.* You obviously know what a girlfriend is. If you don't, put this book down, go watch any romantic comedy ever made, then come back and we'll talk. However, oftentimes you'll hear this term used by a Heterosexual Female referring to another Heterosexual Female or the plural *girlfriends*, referring to an entire group of other Heterosexual Females. No, this does not mean you're speaking to a lesbian;* the Heterosexual Female simply uses these words as a term of endearment** to refer to her closest female friends. The same rule

....

*Lesbians are great, especially Ellen DeGeneres, Rachel Maddow, Rosie O'Donnell, and Queen Latifah's girlfriend.

**Terms of Endearment* is also a *fantastic* movie starring Shirley MacLaine and Debra Winger. In one of Shirley MacLaine's 500 memoirs, she writes about this weird day on set when Debra Winger held her down and farted in her face. It's a *must-read* for all folks who consider themselves part of the human race.

does not apply to the males of the species. If you hear a Heterosexual Male referring to his friend as his boyfriend, he is most certainly not a Heterosexual Male, and if he's cute, please tell him I said hi and to follow me on Instagram.

Old Ball and Chain *noun.* This is another situation in which the words mean something other than what you think. Heterosexuals like to refer to their marital partner as "my old ball and chain" in a sarcastic and humorous tone. *Do not*, under any circumstances, automatically assume that the Heterosexual is referring to S&M sex, as this will *not* go over well at all. Especially if you're talking to your uncle Rob about your aunt Suzanne. Trust me on this one, you guys.

Skort *noun.* Popular among Heterosexual Female tennis players, this is the fashion version of shampoo and conditioner in one bottle, pairing shorts and a skirt into one highly functional and highly unattractive fashion statement.

Sup Another example of Heterosexual verbal efficiency, this word is short for the question "What's up?"—a strange term that was created sometime in the past 50 years as another way of asking, "What's going on with you?" but, like, who has the time to say that many words at once? I certainly don't, and I have *no* life whatsoever.

Talbots *noun.* A clothing store popular among Heterosexual Females in their 50s and 60s. This Heterosexual one-stop shop is the perfect place to get slacks with elastic waists, chunky plastic jewelry, and oversized silk blouses that tell the world, "I'm a grand-mother of three, and I like being comfortable!"*

That Time of the Month *noun.* A term used by Heterosexual Females to politely describe their monthly menstrual cycle. The female might say, "I'm feeling bloated because it's that time of the month," or "I'm having the worst cramps because it's that time of the month," while Heterosexual Males might say, "Put the gun down, Alice. I know it's that time of the month, but I didn't know you had planned on eating that last Double Stuf Oreo!"

The Game *noun.* This term refers to a specific sports game, though the sport itself is never referred to. Instead, a Heterosexual might invite you over by asking, "I'm having some guys over to watch The Game. Wanna come?" Your answer should always be an immediate "No," or else you'll be spending your entire Sunday trying to figure out if all football games have a redeeming halftime show that may or may not feature Madonna, or if that's just the Super Bowl. Spoiler alert: That's just the Super Bowl.

---

*A note on Elderly Heterosexuals: There are many Elderly Heterosexuals out there in the world, and while this book isn't meant to focus on them, I recommend watching the hit television series *The Golden Girls* to learn anything and every-thing about them. Just be prepared to hear Rue McClanahan talk *a lot* about sex in a way that is bound to make you extremely uncomfortable and unsure about growing old.

How to Communicate with a Heterosexual

For the longest time, I wasn't sure how to speak to Heterosexuals. I was constantly worried that I'd say the wrong thing, like asking them, "What is it like to have sexual relations with someone so physically different from you?" or, "Do you *actually* enjoy Showtime's *Homeland*? You can tell me the truth. No one is listening."

Communicating with a Heterosexual isn't nearly as difficult as it seems. There are just some important rules to follow. First and foremost, here is a list of topics to *avoid* while attempting to communicate with a Heterosexual. These topics will be met with dead stares and/or uncomfortable silence:

- Your favorite parts of Diane Keaton's memoir.

- America's marriage/divorce ratio.

- The third season of *The L Word*.

- How Jane Krakowski deserves more respect.

- Sequins.

- The fact that Marilu Henner has that weird disease where she can remember every moment of her life.

- Fog machines and/or disco balls.

- Men's Uggs.

- That super-flamboyant eight-year-old you just discovered on YouTube who sings amazing Lady Gaga covers and calls himself Lady Fierce.

- Michael Kors.

- Glee.

- Any line from the movie *Steel Magnolias*.

The Heterosexual is used to communicating with other Heterosexuals, so when you approach one to start a conversation, try one of these familiar greetings:

- Hey, Jake! Who are your Fantasy Football* picks this year?

....

*Here is how Fantasy Football is described by Wikipedia: "An interactive virtual competition in which people manage professional football players versus one another and that allows people to act as general managers of a pseudo-football team." Still confused? Yeah, I thought so. Basically, you know how you and your friends sit around and imagine what would happen if you made a movie about *The Real Housewives of Beverly Hills* with your fantasy cast and who would play who and what would happen? It's basically like that, except you don't get to imagine how great Kristin Chenoweth or Melissa Leo would be at playing Kim Richards.

- Natalie, you're too skinny!

- You've seen *Knocked Up*, right?

- How's my dawg?!

- I wasn't sure about Lena Dunham, but then I was like, wow! she gets me.

- Want a beer?

- Yo, bro!

- Sorry I'm late. Dealing with my mother-in-law.

Conversing with a Heterosexual Male

Prepare to exit your comfort zone; you are now entering Heterosexual territory. To help you along, I've dramatized an assortment of possible conversations with Heterosexuals.

Non-Heterosexual: Hello, Gary.
Heterosexual Male: Hi, Richard. How are you?
Non-Heterosexual: I'm well! I just got done watching the first season of *Ally McBeal* on Netflix streaming.

(The Heterosexual scratches his head and stands awkwardly, not saying anything. The Non-Heterosexual can either remain silent, run away, or offer one of the following changes of subject.)

"But you know who's great? Gavin DeGraw."
"Hey, did I tell you my sister-in-law is pregnant again?"
Or the always dependable: "Could you go for some wings?"

In the instance above, the Non-Heterosexual got himself into a predicament by immediately mentioning something the Heterosexual wouldn't relate to. Sometimes the Heterosexual causes the problem from the get-go. Either way, when dealing with Heterosexuals, you should *always* be prepared to eat at least 12 wings.

On Sports

Heterosexual: Hey, Richard. Did you see Derek Jeter on *Leno* last night?

Now, in this situation, the Heterosexual has definitely thrown you a curveball. Not only do you not watch Jay Leno, but you also have absolutely *no* idea who Derek Jeter is. You can either (A) admit you have no idea what he's talking about, (B) lie and say, "Yes, Jay is *such* a riot," or (C) use your phone to google Mr. Jeter and discover that he's the guy who was rumored to be dating Madonna for, like, two days back in 2006. However, when doing the latter, your attempts to steer the conversation toward discussing Madonna's black hair in *A League of Their Own* are highly discouraged.

Conversing with a Heterosexual Female

Conversations with the Heterosexual Female can be a bit trickier. She is more likely to solicit advice or opinions, so be prepared or things could go terribly wrong.

On Clothing

Heterosexual Female: Hey, Richard. Do you like this shirt?

Non-Heterosexual: Sure, it's cute.

Heterosexual Female: But like, is it just cute or is it hot? I want to look really good for my date with Max tonight.

Non-Heterosexual: Yeah, it's hot.

Heterosexual Female: Are you sure? I feel like the blue one might be hotter.

Time-out! You may not know it, but you're walking into a conversational land mine. The fate of this Heterosexual Female's night is in *your* hands, and if it doesn't live up to expectations, you could potentially be blamed for an unsuccessful date, a lifetime of loneliness, or the cold she caught because you didn't suggest that she wear a sweater. Your answer should be:

Non-Heterosexual: Yeah. Go with the blue.

Heterosexual Female: So this one looks bad?

See how she got you there? *Do not*, under any circumstances, answer, "Yes, that one looks bad." *Never* and I repeat *never* tell a Heterosexual Female that she looks bad.

Non-Heterosexual: No. I love this one, but I also love the blue.
Heterosexual Female: But you think this one isn't as sexy?
Non-Heterosexual: No, I think they're both sexy.
Heterosexual Female: Now I feel like you're just saying that.

She's now backed you into a corner, and there are only two ways to respond: (A) Negate everything by saying, "I was wrong. The blue is perfect. You *have* to wear it" or (B) "I saw Sofía Vergara wear something just like that in *People* magazine."

Heterosexual Female: Oh. Are you sure?

At this point, no matter what you've just told her, you should quickly nod with a look of deep concentration and say, "Yes. I've never been more sure of anything in my entire life."

On Guys

The Heterosexual Female will most likely come to you with concern over the Heterosexual Male in her life. You may be thinking, "Oh! That's easy! I give great dating advice." But don't forget that the Heterosexual Female's dating patterns are very different from anyone else's, and must be discussed with the kind of skill and focus reserved for open-heart surgery or writing a really good musical comedy like *Guys and Dolls* or *High School Musical 3*.

Heterosexual Female: Hey, can I talk to you?

Always answer *yes* here. If you say *no*, you'll spend more time explaining why than you would have listening to what she needed to say in the first place. I don't care what time your therapist appointment is.

Non-Heterosexual: Of course, Amber. What's up?
Heterosexual Female: You know that guy I've been seeing?

At this point, you might be inspired to ask, "Which one?" as Amber is "that kind of girl," but avoid any such statement, as this will result in an hourlong discussion as to whether or not you think Amber is a slut. Maybe you *do* think Amber is a slut, maybe Amber thinks she's a slut, and, let's be honest, maybe Amber *is* a slut, but the last thing she needs is her friend Jeffery pointing that out. Especially since Jeffery is a slut, too.

Non-Heterosexual: Sure. What about him?
Heterosexual Female: Well, we had this amazing night last weekend. We went to the modern art museum, and we had this fabulous dinner, but then, after he left the next morning, I never heard from him again. And that was over a week ago.

We all know what's going on here—even Amber, though she doesn't want to admit it. This guy wasn't looking to date Amber, and there's about zero chance she's going to hear from him again until she bumps into him at a New Year's Eve party two years from now and makes the same mistake all over again. But you, her friend, shouldn't say this. I don't care how many people bought *He's Just Not That into You*; nobody, especially your Heterosexual Female friend, wants to hear that. Instead, you should say:

Non-Heterosexual: Can I be honest with you, Amber?
Heterosexual Female: Yes.
Non-Heterosexual: I didn't want to tell you because I love you, but I got a really, really weird vibe from that guy.

At this point, Amber will be shocked, but, even better, distracted. She thought this guy was the love of her life, and it is best not to go into any details on your theory, as it will only hurt her even further, and, more importantly, you still have no idea which guy you're talking about.

Heterosexual Female: Oh my God. Like how?

This is where it's going to get tough, but here are five ways to answer and wrap up the conversation in one swift move.

1. "He just seems, I don't know, shady."

2. "He gave my friend Stacey crabs." This will work even if your Heterosexual friend knows your other friend Stacey, as, let's face it, anybody with a name like *Stacey* has probably had crabs.
3. "I'm pretty sure I made out with him in college."
4. "Oh gurl, you don't even want to *know!*" This one works best if you wave your hands around on "Oh gurl."
5. Or, tap your nostril, look around as if you're being watched, then mouth "coke."

Communicating with a Heterosexual is one of the trickiest parts of the Heterosexual-Watching process. However, if you have an open mind and, undoubtedly, at some point can discuss NASCAR or the latest *Resident Evil* movie, or in the case of the Heterosexual Female, discuss how smug she thinks Taylor Swift seems, you will be completely and totally prepared.

Now we're nearing the end of this book, and our precious time together. You've learned a lot so far, and I know what you're probably beginning to ask yourself: "Am I a Heterosexual?!?"

Shhh. Why so panicked? If there's anything I've taught you thus far, it's that being a Heterosexual is *totally* OK. It's 100 percent natural and nowadays wholeheartedly accepted. Honestly. Some Heterosexuals have gone on to do great things, and to any Heterosexuals out there struggling with who they are, I promise you that it does get better.

It doesn't have to be so hard to determine whether or not you are a Heterosexual. In fact, you could just ask yourself the questions in this next quiz, the last section of our Heterosexual SATs.

The Heterosexual SAT #5:
Am I a Heterosexual?

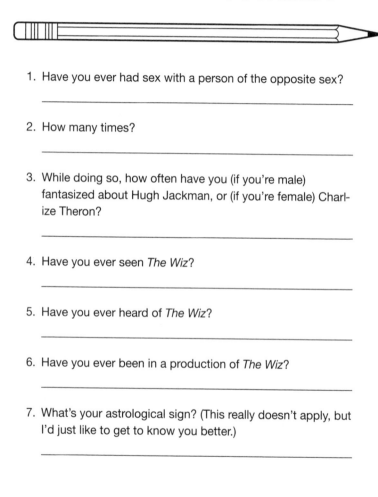

1. Have you ever had sex with a person of the opposite sex?

   _____

2. How many times?

   _____

3. While doing so, how often have you (if you're male) fantasized about Hugh Jackman, or (if you're female) Charlize Theron?

   _____

4. Have you ever seen *The Wiz*?

   _____

5. Have you ever heard of *The Wiz*?

   _____

6. Have you ever been in a production of *The Wiz*?

   _____

7. What's your astrological sign? (This really doesn't apply, but I'd just like to get to know you better.)

   _____

8. Which is your favorite NFL team?

   _____

9. If you don't watch football, explain why.

   _____

10. Do you often think about that scene in *The First Wives Club* when they fall 50 stories in a window-washing platform?

    _____

11. But do you prefer the scene in *The First Wives Club* where Bette Midler pours all of Goldie Hawn's liquor down the sink?

    _____

12. If you're male: Who's your favorite Victoria's Secret model? If you're female: What are your thoughts on Mark Ruffalo?

    _____

13. Have you ever used the phrase *I can't, I have rehearsal* in reference to either community theater or modern dance?

    _____

14. Look at your Facebook profile and count how many pictures you have of yourself wearing a beret.

    _____

15. Who is Emmitt Smith?

    _____

16. Have you ever heard of the TV show *Hillbilly Hand Fishin'*?

   _____

17. When you think of Sharon Stone, do you think of how she didn't do much of anything but host AIDS fundraisers throughout the late 1990s?

   _____

18. When you refer to Academy Award–winning screenwriter Dustin Lance Black, do you use his full name or the hyperpersonal Lance?

   _____

19. Who won *Project Runway* in 2010?

   _____

20. Who's your favorite Mama Rose in *Gypsy*? (Again, just curious.)

   _____

ANSWERS:

If you answered *yes* to question 1, you are a Heterosexual.

If you answered 0 to question 2, you are definitely *not* a Heterosexual.

If you answered 0 to question 3, you are most definitely a Heterosexual.

If you have been deemed a Heterosexual by question 3 and have also answered *yes* to questions 4 and 5, you simply have great taste.

If you answered *yes* to question 6, who did you play, and is there video footage? Call me and let me know.

If you can answer question 8, you are most likely a Heterosexual.

If you answered anything but "I prefer baseball" to question 9, you're probably *not* a Heterosexual.

If you answered *yes* to questions 10 and 11, you are *not* a Heterosexual.

If you can answer question 12, you're a Heterosexual.

If you answered *yes* to question 13, you are *not* a Heterosexual.

If you answered anything more than "once, but it was on a dare" to question 14, you are *not* a Heterosexual.

The correct answer to question 15: A very famous former NFL football player. And knowing that, obviously makes you a Heterosexual.

If you answered *yes* to question 16, you are a Heterosexual with suspicious taste.

If you answered yes to question 17, you are *not* a Heterosexual.

If you can answer question 18, you are as gay as they come, and you probably know movie director Bryan Singer, too. And me, now that I think about it.

If you know the answer to question 19, you are a female.

Question 20 has no right or wrong answer, unless you said the made-for-TV version with Bette Midler, in which case: Ew.

And, finally, if you're too confused, tired, or lazy to figure out this quiz (and I don't blame you), rip out this page and use it to make a paper football. If you know how to do this, you are a Heterosexual.

In Closing

Afterthoughts about Heterosexuals

WOW! HAVE WE COVERED A LOT OF GROUND OR WHAT?!

If you've actually been reading this and not just standing at the books table in the store and flipping through the pages while your girlfriend tries on pants (which if you *really* want to impress her are most likely called "straight-leg fit" or "skinny," but stop there on the pant descriptions or else your girlfriend will assume I've turned you gay), you've learned about Heterosexual Habitats, Feeding Patterns, and even Kenny G!

Of course, there are many things native to the Heterosexual and his/her lifestyle that I did not have room to include in detail, and, sure, I could save these omissions for my second Heterosexual-Watching spotter's guide, but you know what? That would be lazy and not giving you the full experience. Like going to see Christina Aguilera in concert and not hearing "Beautiful," because ol' Christina decided she should save it for next time. *No*, Christina Aguilera. I came to see you, and by doing so, expect to hear "Beautiful." Do you think I came all the way to Boston to hear songs from your *Bionic Woman* album? No, I did not.

It's wrong not to give people what they came for in totality, so here, my dear, lovely, attractive, and, might I add, delicious-smelling readers is a list of things you should definitely know about Heterosexuals.

Boy Bands

It is a common misconception that the popularity of boy bands is based solely on teenage girls. While teenage girls are a very large portion of their fan base, the most popular boy bands would be nowhere today without the enthusiasm of adult Heterosexual Females who are *way* too old to be screaming for a 16-year-old boy who looks a lot like Ellen DeGeneres. Boy bands remind adult Heterosexual Females of simpler times when love meant writing someone's name on your binder, and not screaming at each other in the middle of IKEA over a bed whose name you can't pronounce, like Fjellse.

Everybody Loves Raymond

This is one of the most popular shows among Heterosexuals. It is a half-hour comedy program starring Ray Romano and Patricia Heaton. If you've ever spent a weekend with your parents, you've undoubtedly sat through at least five episodes of this show. First-time Heterosexual Watchers are constantly asking me questions about it, questions like, "Does everyone *actually* love Raymond?" The answer is *yes*, but it is more complicated than that. Raymond is a fictional character, so it is a lot easier for him to be loved by everyone than, say, me. For example, Raymond doesn't have to worry about book deadlines, paying off his student loans, or wondering why Frankie Muniz has more Twitter followers than him when Frankie Muniz hasn't been on TV in years, and I've been on TV multiple times this year and try really, really hard to get people, especially on Twitter, to follow me. So, yeah. The short answer is that everybody does love Raymond, but the long answer is a lot more complicated and is best not to think about too hard.

Guyliner Versus Eyeliner

Heterosexual Males involved in the subset of punk or emo* will often sport guyliner. Guyliner is just regular eyeliner, commonly worn by females, but with Heterosexual Males, they felt the need to create their own term, lest they be seen as cross-dressers. However, guyliner is just eyeliner being called something else. Do not let this confuse you. Also, do not wear guyliner. It is *so* 2010.

Emo comes from the term *emotional hard-core*, which, if you think about it, is also a great way to describe Dr. Phil. When speaking to Emo Heterosexuals, never, under any circumstances, suggest that *emo* is just *Elmo* without the *L*. They will *not* be amused, no matter how funny your Elmo impression is.

Pretending to Have Seen *Citizen Kane*

Film buffs have deemed *Citizen Kane* the greatest movie of all time. While acknowledging a world where New Year's Eve exists, I beg to differ; you can't deny the popularity and strange reverence for this movie that, despite how many times I've watched it, I still can't figure out what it is about. Heterosexuals are expected to have seen this movie, and the majority have not. However, almost all Heterosexuals you know will claim not only to have seen it, but also that it is one of their all-time favorite movies, next to *Avatar* and *She's All That*.

Listening to Adele and Crying Behind Closed Doors

Here is a staggering statistic for you: *All* the Heterosexuals you know have at some point in the past year closed the door to their home or bedroom and listened to Adele's "Someone Like You" and openly wept to themselves.

Sporks

A spoon and fork combined, and frankly, one of the greatest inventions in Heterosexual history.

Throwing Drinks in People's Faces

Based solely on what I've learned from watching basically every reality show of the past decade, Heterosexual Females love to throw drinks in people's faces when they're upset. It is the Heterosexual Female's way of aggressively and physically stating that she does *not* appreciate whatever has just been said or done to her. I've never had a drink thrown in my face, but perhaps after that massive generalization I will. I applaud the Heterosexual Female; I only worry about those countless wasted cocktails.

The Black Eyed Peas
This actually covers two things beloved by Heterosexuals. First, of course, is the food, a dish Heterosexuals traditionally eat on New Year's Eve or Rosh Hashanah to bring good luck. And second, the band of the same name featuring Will.I.Am, Fergie, and some other guys whose names no one can even pretend to remember. I've never been much of a Black Eyed Peas fan myself; however, once I heard the true story of Fergie peeing her pants onstage at a concert, my appreciation for this pop band most certainly shifted toward the positive.

Breaking Bad
Even though it's a TV show about meth—which isn't something you get to say a lot these days now that Paula Abdul isn't on *American Idol*—Heterosexuals are surprisingly addicted to this show, almost as intensely as if it were, well, meth.

Having Gay Friends
These days, every Heterosexual has a gay friend. Gay friends are the new black. And a black gay friend? Well, that's just the holy grail. Heterosexuals love spending time with their gay friends, because it's a nice opportunity not to worry about the lingering

sexual tension that is likely to exist between them and their friends of the opposite sex, and an even nicer opportunity to talk about whatever has recently happened on *The Real Housewives* of anywhere.* If I were a bit smarter and a lot less lazy, I would start a service called Rent-A-Gay, which, despite how it sounds, would have nothing to do with male escorts, but would be a rental-style program where Heterosexuals in need of some gay friend companionship could rent a gay friend for the day, the week, or, in special cases, the month. I guess what I'm saying is, I'm available and take MasterCard.

This is a world full of wonderful Heterosexuals, and all you need to do is take a moment, stop, look around you, and take them all in. Perhaps you'll learn a little something; perhaps you'll make a great new friend; perhaps you'll better understand the friends you already have; perhaps you'll figure out something to talk to your sister Sarah-Ann about, or your brother Bart, or perhaps you'll finally watch *Titanic* and realize that—you know what, Heterosexuals are right—hearts really do go on.

With this spotter's guide, I hope I've inspired a sense of adventure in you. A sense to open your mind to a wonderful species of humans that, up until this book, have only been found in most movies, every single television show in history,

---

*Why haven't they made *The Real Housewives of the Afterlife* a show on the Syfy network?

music, art, magazines, pretty much any public place all over the world, and most other books besides this one and those written by Armistead Maupin.

So put this book down, leave your iPhone at home, grab some binoculars, put on a comfortable pair of shoes (but still make them cute, like a fun hiking boot or some trendy sneakers; I'm not suggesting you turn into a barbarian), open your mind to the variety of the world, and start Heterosexual Watching.

Acknowledgments

Jordana Tusman, my editor, who always knew the right time to say "maybe less *Grey Gardens* references." Scott Mendel, for convincing me I could write this. Julie Klausner, for introducing me to Scott Mendel. My very awesome boyfriend who makes life a lot better. My very talented friends who inspire me: Cole Escola, Bryan Safi, Drew Droege, Jim Hansen, Erin Markey, Max Steele, Eric Gilliland, Ben Rimalower, Billy Eichner, Guy Branum, Louis Virtel, Michael Arden, and Rachel Shukert.

The fine folks at Commissary Coffee in Los Angeles where most of this book was written. And anybody who has ever shared one of my YouTube videos, tweets, or blog posts: thanks for making me feel cool enough to actually do this.

FIELDNOTES

Washington Park Library - PCL

FIELDNOTES